WHAT'S A MOTHER TO DO?

MARLENE OBIE

HARVEST HOUSE PUBLISHERS
Eugene, Oregon 97402

All Scripture quotations in this book are taken from the Revised Standard Version of the Bible, Copyright © 1946, 1952, 1971 by the Division of Christian Education of the National Council of the Churches of Christ in the United States of America. Used by permission.

WHAT'S A MOTHER TO DO?

Introduction

I have always been a believer in romance, fairy tales, and happy endings. So it wasn't surprising that I entered into marriage and motherhood with some pretty unrealistic attitudes.

As I held each of my newborn babies in my arms I vowed to God and myself to give them lots of love, raise them to be responsible people, and inspire them to be good Christians. I was convinced that if I loved them enough there would never be a problem. As we together moved through the various stages of their childhood I kept on convincing myself that their success and happiness was dependent on my performance as a mother.

You can imagine my surprise, shock, and disappointment when my children began to exhibit the same characteristics as their peers. I consulted a number of Christian and secular psychology books and concluded that I had committed irreversable errors. I had a picture in my mind of the perfect Christian family and mine was a poor imitation. I wondered what had happened. I had devoted most of my life to my children. Wasn't that enough?

I was sure any flaws in my children's personalities were my fault. I hadn't been a good enough Christian—I had either been too permissive or too rigid—I had not washed their diapers in the right soap and had allowed them to destroy their brains by eating too much sugar. The list of my sins was long enough to hang me and the resulting guilt stood ready to spring the trap door.

I felt completely alone in my despair. As I looked around me I saw families that appeared to have it all together. Hence I didn't feel free to open up. Little did I know that these other mothers were going through the same ordeals and doubts.

It was only as I began to talk over my frustrations with my Heavenly Father that I was able to cope. I gave these hopes and fears and confusion to Him and He filled me with forgiveness for my inadequacies, release from guilt, and the realization that my children were responsible for their own actions. He also gave me the courage to begin to talk to other women who revealed the same inner agonies I had. Finally, He enabled me to laugh at our family foibles. This has been one of the basic contributions to my emotional survival. It only hurts when I don't laugh.

I have written down these prayer conversations in order to encourage others to take their pain and anger and fears to the Greatest Psychologist of all time. I have confidence that he will lead us to whatever solutions there are. He is also the Father of our children and He cares for them as deeply as He cares for us.

The Bible verses I have used are the ones that give me daily hope and comfort. I have made a point of underlining in my Bible the words that give me the strength to meet each new day.

I apologize to my children for any embarrassment I may have caused them by revealing their faults to the public. I hope they'll look at my overall purpose to help other parents in pain and forgive me. Despite the pain, worry, anger, and disappointment they have caused me at times they have brought tremendous joy into my life.

I thank the Lord that He has enabled me to share my life with these special three young people I call my children and with my husband, and that He has endowed us all with the love and sense of humor we need to coexist.

I look forward to a time when our differences will be inconsequential, and our love for each other will result in a lasting peace. I hope it happens in my lifetime.

A Mother's Insomnia

Father, it's three o'clock in the morning, and my son isn't home yet. I've been lying here for hours listening intently for the car in the driveway and the click of the lock as he tries to slip in without being heard.

I know my prayers are repetitious, Lord. Again and again I've asked You to protect him from harm and danger. I don't mean to be double-minded, Lord. I *am* praying with faith; take away the pain of fear that's lodged in my stomach.

At first I was annoyed at my son's thoughtlessness. Then I became angry with him for putting me through this. Now I'm afraid the phone *will* ring, and I'll be told he's been in an accident or is in jail.

Send Your angels to surround the car, Lord, and bring it safely home. Meanwhile, keep him out of the clutches of the evil one. If he is doing something he shouldn't be, speak to him through his conscience. Drown out the voices of temptation and help him to stay out of trouble.

There! Was that a car door I heard? Yes, it's him. Thank You, Lord. Now maybe I can get some sleep.

What now? Should I confront him and demand an explanation? All that would do is wake up the rest of the family. I'll just sit up in bed so he'll see me as he goes by our room, and he'll know I'm aware of when he came in. The rest will keep until morning.

Now I can sleep, Lord, knowing my family is safe.

Everyone's accounted for. Good night and thank You again for Your assistance.

Thou has kept count of my tossings; put thou my tears in thy bottle! Are they not in thy book?

Psalm 56:8

I do not pray that thou shouldst take them out of the world, but that thou shouldst keep them from the evil one.

John 17:15

Mixed Blessings

They did it again, Lord! Just when I think I have my children pegged, they surprise me and change personalities.

I've learned not to act smug when they exhibit extraordinary brainpower, musical talent, or Christian compassion for others, because the odds are 50 to 1 that they'll follow up with some action that will make me feel they have regressed to preschool age.

I had accepted the fact that these kids I live with are selfish, sloppy, lazy, spoiled, and stubborn. I was sure they would never amount to anything, but look at them now.

Gene actually called to let me know where he is and when he'll be home, Tim mowed the lawn without being nagged, and Lana cleaned the house before I got home from work today! I had to go out and check the house number to be sure I was in the right place. In addition to these surprises, everyone was home for supper at the same time, and they all liked the meal!

As I looked around the table I realized how lucky I am to have three healthy, normal children. I know I grumble a lot about their faults, but I notice their virtues, too. Help me to tell them more often that I think they are neat kids. Keep me from constantly picking at them; stifle my nagging tongue.

Many people today are deciding not to start families, and others claim they regret having children. While I understand these feelings I cannot agree with them.

My life has been blessed over and over through my children. The last 20 years have been filled with laughter, tears, hopes, worries, pride, and anger. It's never been boring—that's for sure. But You know, Lord, I wouldnt't trade even the worst times for a life without children. Whether the time ahead is good or bad, I will remain thankful I'm a mother.

Oops, there's an argument in progress. The lull is over. I'm home, all right!

Lo, sons are a heritage from the Lord, the fruit of the womb a reward. Like the arrows in the hand of a warrior are the sons of one's youth. Happy is the man who has his quiver full of them! He shall not be put to shame when he speaks with his enemies in the gate.

Psalm 127:3-5

Wake-Up Calls

Father, I really don't think I'm cut out to be a wake-up alarm. You know what a hard time I have just getting *myself* up each morning! Well, I realize it's my motherly duty to get the kids off to school, but don't expect me to be cheerful about it, especially when it comes to evicting my oldest child from his bed.

Although he has an aversion to sleep before 3:00 A.M. he embraces it tightly until 2:00 P.M. When he was in high school we got trapped in this tug-of-war, and we still keep playing the silly game. I have to nag, nag, nag, or he won't get to work on time. He just shuts off his alarm and depends on me to get him up. Then he gets belligerent about *my* attitude. By the time I've called, prodded, pleaded, and screamed at him to get up I feel like the Shrew of the Year. Many times I've ended the battle in tears. I hate this, Lord! What can I do?

I can give the problem to You, but can I keep from interfering? He can't afford to lose his job.

Forgive my doubt, Lord. I release this problem to You now. I know You want what's best for my son and that You know what he needs. Tomorrow I will keep my mouth shut and let him get up on his own or suffer the consequences. Help him, Lord, to live up to his responsibilities, and help me to let go.

How long will you lie there, O sluggard? When will you arise from your sleep? A little sleep, a little slumber, a little folding of the hands to rest, and poverty will come upon you like a vagabond, and want like an armed man.

Proverbs 6:9-11

Family Evangelism

I don't understand, Lord.

Many years ago as a young child I sat alone in church without a family around me. Now here I am again by myself in Your church.

I took my duty to teach my children Your ways seriously. When they were younger we came to worship as a family unit.

It wasn't always easy. After pushing and nagging everyone to get up, put dress clothes on, and hurry, hurry, I often breathed a large sigh as we took our seats in the sanctuary, relieved that we had made it on time and in a fairly presentable state.

In later years our home was in a state of unrest (to say the least) on Sunday mornings. It sometimes took bribes, loud voices, threats, and tears to accomplish my mission of evangelism.

Was it worth all the trouble, Lord? It's much calmer since my children reached the "age of choice." Now I ask calmly, "Who's going to church?" and my daughter frequently accompanies me. (Forgive the snide remarks I sometimes make to my sons.)

I worry about the others. I have failed to give them a strong faith in You.

What more can I do, Lord?

I can refrain from launching into fire-and-brimstone sermons, and I can love them as You do — forgiving, forbearing, and waiting.

I can be thankful they have not rejected You. It's true that they cannot sit on the fence forever, but I can go on praying that they'll fall in the right direction. Many Christian women I know have indicated that their children refuse to acknowledge Your existence and will not even discuss religion. My children believe You *are* but have not yet learned that the walk through life is upbeat when they walk at Your side. They have acquired knowledge of the head, not of the heart.

I have to accept the fact that my area of responsibility has boundaries. I cannot choose for my children. I cannot *give* them faith; they have to take it.

I can believe that You love them and will call them, and that they will respond in due time.

Thank You for helping me to understand and for lifting the load of guilt that was dragging me down.

My son, if your heart is wise, my heart too will be glad.

Proverbs 23:15

From there you will seek the Lord your God, and you will find him, if you search after him with all your heart and with all your soul.

Deuteronomy 4:29

Mirages

Lord, I'm envious of people who have more money than we do to spend on our kids.

Maybe we could have had more luxuries if I had gone to work sooner. I always thought I was right to stay home when the children were younger, but now I wonder if I cheated them by not earning money to buy the material things they craved.

Perhaps we could have bought a bigger house, a swimming pool, or nicer cars. A membership at the country club might have improved their social standing. More-frequent family vacations probably would have brought us closer together.

Money seems to disappear as fast as we earn it. There's always another bill to pay or groceries we need. Will we ever have enough, Lord?

Sometimes it seems like all my kids ever do is gripe. I'm tired of hearing about kids who have received their first car as a present along with all the spending money they need for recreation and gas. I'd like to be able to buy them expensive clothes and give them private tennis lessons.

Actually we don't do all that badly. They are wearing the "in" brand of tennis shoes and jeans, although they may not have as many pairs as some kids. I remember the foster children we had who came to us with one pair of jeans apiece and one change of underwear and socks in a paper bag. Why do my children always look at the families that have more than we do instead of those that have less?

Money doesn't guarantee happiness. It doesn't

protect families from divorce or parent-child problems or bad health. It would be nice to have more,
but You have given us riches that last, Lord. Help
us to be more appreciative. We have more than
enough food to eat, a roof over our heads, and
each other. Best of all, we have Your constant love.
We're millionaires after all!

There is great gain in godliness with content-
ment; for we brought nothing into the world,
and we cannot take anything out of the world;
but if we have food and clothing, with these
we shall be content.

1 Timothy 6:6-8

A Prayer for Peace

Whose children are these, Lord? They can't possibly be mine! There must be some terrible mistake. I think some alien beings must have invaded my home and taken over my children's bodies.

Just listen to that noise! They argue over everything: what TV program to watch, whose turn it is to help in the kitchen, or who gets to drive to the store.

If there's a way to solve this battle over the bathroom, I wish You'd show it to me. I've considered posting a rotating schedule for baths, but there would still be someone trying to brush his teeth while someone else is washing her hair in the bathroom sink. The first sounds I hear in the morning are of three young people in the bathroom pushing each other away from the sink and fighting over the hair dryer. I could scream! And I frequently do.

You know I've always been a peacemaker. So where did these trained guerilla fighters come from?

I can't believe the language they use when they're yelling at each other. Wherever did they learn that profanity? I taught them not to swear, and I always set a good example; well, nearly always.

I recently heard that parents are supposed to walk away and let their kids fight, that they really won't hurt each other. Whoever thought up that gem of wisdom hasn't seen my son and daughter scratching and punching!

If I lose my temper, I only add more sound effects to the scene. Help me, Lord, to be a wise and fair arbitrator. Show me how to keep my cool and discuss the problems calmly with them, listening to all sides.

Make them aware of the need to practice Your Golden Rule more often.

Bestow on us Your peace, Lord.

Psalm 120:6,7

Letting Go

Dear Lord, I give this child to You again. I know I've done this many times in the last 20 years. Despite my good intentions I keep grabbing the reins away from You and trying to steer him my way.

You'd think I would have learned by now that I can't nag this young man into responsibility. The thought keeps haunting me that it's my fault that he's taking so long to grow up. Perhaps I failed to demand enough of him when he was younger. Also, I'm sure he inherited his skill of procrastination from me. I know I can't go back and change all that now, and at his age I can't make him follow my advice.

I want so much for him to succeed at something worthwhile. His self-image needs a boost. Okay, I admit I'd like to be able to brag a little, too. After listening to other mothers reel off their children's accomplishments since graduation, I find it difficult to explain what my son is doing. I suppose I could say he's into employment-market research. Actually he's studying to be idle rich, but so far he's mastered only the idle part. Father, forgive my envy. Help me to accept him the way he is now.

You know I've always loved him, and I always will, no matter what. But now I must learn to love him in a different way. Although he physically left the nest several months ago, my emotional apron strings have not been cut. Help me to let go with grace, Lord. Seal my mouth from telling him what kind of job to get, what to eat, or how to spend his money.

Thank You for being so patient with me. I give my son to You with complete trust. I'm sure You know a lot more about raising children than I do. You've had a lot more experience.

I have been young, and now am old; yet I have not seen the righteous forsaken or his children begging bread. He is ever giving liberally and lending, and his children become a blessing.
Psalm 37:25,26

A Daughter's Moods

Help me to be kind and understanding with my daughter, Lord. She's in a terrible mood tonight. I came home from work today and found her moping around the house with a long, expressionless face. Attempts by her father and brother and me to converse with her were met with blank stares and curt, one-syllable words. I tried to find out what was bothering her, but she just snapped at me. I was irritated with her behavior and made some sarcastic remarks.

I realize it isn't fair to expect her to always be smiling and sweet. I need to accept her moods, just as I expect her to tolerate mine.

I can remember well the agonies of being 15, and I sympathize with her feelings. She considers herself unattractive and cannot believe that her acne is only temporary or that the distribution of her weight will change.

She also has felt deserted by her friends this summer. They've all been busy and have not included her very much in their activities. How well I know the pain of being left out! I wish I could just make the pain go away by holding her tight, as I did when she was a little girl. It was a lot easier to doctor skinned knees!

I'm concerned about her feeling of hopelessness, Lord. Not long ago she asked me if anything good was ever going to happen to her. I tried to point out all the blessings she had received, but I don't think it helped much.

She wants to be accepted, Lord, in the special

choir, the basketball team, or the dance team. I know she's expressed these desires to You. I add my prayers to hers and ask that You help her to achieve those goals that You know will bring real happiness. Only You know which ones are for her ultimate good.

I'm sometimes afraid that if she fails to gain recognition in wholesome ways she may resort to less-desirable methods of obtaining attention from her peers. Guide her down the paths that You have chosen for her. Fitting in with the popular crowd is not important. I know that now, but I didn't at her age. She needs a few close Christian friends who like her the way she is. That's all that any of us need, isn't it.?

She'll soon outgrow this distressing age. In the meantime, let me be gentle with her. Guard my tongue from speaking harsh words when she takes her frustrations out on me. Let me help her to find confidence in herself and faith in Your love for her.

A soft answer turns away wrath, but a harsh word stirs up anger.
Proverbs 15:1

I know the plans I have for you, says the Lord, plans for welfare and not for evil, to give you a future and a hope.
Jeremiah 29:11

Mrs. In-Between

Lord, help! I'm caught between two people I love —my husband and my son. Their fighting is tearing me apart.

They are alike in many ways, which is why they communicate so poorly. They are both too busy talking to listen.

I can see both sides clearly. My husband wants our son to grow up and be independent, but he keeps trying to force his ideas on our son. He always comes on too strong, and he refuses to be more diplomatic. I understand my husband's frustrations and share them, but my head tells me that we have to let our son stumble and fall sometimes.

My son wants to be free to live his own life, but he won't take the necessary steps to break away. Legally he's an adult, but emotionally he's still a rebellious child who wants the security of being cared for. He expects our help when he can't fulfill his responsibilities, but he's annoyed when we ask for his assistance. I'm sympathetic to his feelings and I'm truly worried about his future.

Arguments have become a daily fare in our home. The battles between my husband and son generally bring me into the middle. As I try to explain my son to my husband and vice versa, I end up fighting with both of them. Their stubbornness exasperates me, Lord. My husband blames me for my son's behavior, and my son dislikes me for getting on his case. I just can't win for losing!

Father, please take this burden from me. I cannot

bear the responsibility of being a one-woman peacekeeping team.

Beneath all the anger and bitterness lies genuine love. Lord, fan that flicker into a full flame that will consume the minor irritations. Let their actions be guided by their love of each other.

Forgive us all, Lord, for not remembering to bring our problems to You so we might receive the wisdom we need to solve them.

> Children, obey your parents in the Lord, for this is right. "Honor your father and mother" (this is the first commandment with a promise), "that it may be well with you and that you may live long on the earth." Fathers, do not provoke your children to anger, but bring them up in the discipline and instruction of the Lord.
>
> Ephesians 6:1-4

In the Middle

Lord, am I guilty of failing to show my middle child how much I love and appreciate him? I used to scorn as pure nonsense the psychological studies that link a child's personality to his placement in the family. Could they be right?

I sometimes wonder if my son's frequent use of profanity is his way of attracting attention. He knows I'll respond immediately. His lack of self-confidence and short temper also concern me deeply. He may be sending out signals to say he feels unloved.

He's really a good kid. He studies hard and gets good grades, and he's conscientious about doing his work except for cleaning his room and taking out the garbage. As he often reminds me, "Nobody's perfect!" Unlike other teenagers, he doesn't seek the favor of his peers. He is content with a few friends.

"As I see it," he once related, "the more social you are, the easier it is to get into trouble."

There are times when I'm doubtful if this serious young man was really once that mischievous little imp who ran full-throttle through every day as a preschooler. Now he's quite content to read, watch TV, or play games with a friend.

I need to find more time to spend alone with him, to develop a lasting friendship. With two children who are always on the go and into many activities, the quiet stay-at-home body can be ignored.

It seems like we've just begun to know each other while we've been going to football games and races together this year and arguing about politics and religion. With only a year left of school, he'll soon be gone.

You'll have to take over now, Lord. I know he doesn't always believe in You the same way I do. He's seeking to understand You intellectually, but he assures me he does believe You're there. I'm sure his faith will change and become stronger as he grows older and experiences more of life's lessons. However far he may wander, I know he'll come back to You, and I trust You to guard and protect him.

Thank You for loaning me this special child.

Do not withhold good from those to whom it is due, when it is in your power to do it.

Proverbs 3:27

Other People's Kids

Father, have You ever noticed how other people's kids behave in church?

As I sit here observing well-behaved children all around me I'm puzzled as to where these adorable cherubs came from and why my children did not receive their angelic countenances.

Other people's babies drink their bottles, sleep, or silently look around. My babies fussed, babbled loudly, made unmentionable noises, and spit up all over my coat.

Other people's toddlers sit quietly through the service, sometimes drawing masterpieces on the church bulletin. My toddlers squirmed constantly, slammed their hymnbooks shut, and scribbled noisily on the visitors' registration cards. Before our church had carpeting and padded pews, the section where the Obies sat was audibly apparent. It was where chairs were scraping, books were dropping on the floor, and "shhh" was a common sound. My husband and I sat at opposite ends of the aisle to keep our little ones from escaping. They protested loudly when they were restrained from running away. They usually clustered around their dad, checking his suit pockets for gum or Life-savers or giving him a loud smacking kiss on the cheek. I was busy playing the "mean mother" by directing stern scowls at them.

As they moved into their grade-school years my children joined others sitting with the Cherub Choir, where they spent most of the hour wiggling and whispering. They were careful not to look behind them lest they see my raised eyebrows and shaking head.

By the time my kids reached their teens I had to pull them out of bed, prod them into dressing, and literally push them into the car on Sunday morning. Other people's kids walked into church smiling and looking like they belonged on soap or shampoo commercials, while my male offspring considered it a violation of their civil rights to drag a comb through their hair. The jeans they chose to wear had been silently disintegrating in some obscure corner of their room. I was forced to accept their strange appearance or walk into the service late. So I uttered a quick prayer asking You to look beyond their disheveled appearance. (I have to separate my daughter from the rest of the crowd at this point. She *never* leaves the house unless every hair is in place. She would slide to the end of the pew and pretend she didn't know us.)

One of my sons sat in the pew with a morose pout on his face. He was seething with anger at me for rousing him from sleep. My other son tried to hide behind a book the whole hour amid jabs from my elbow and admonitions to listen to the sermon. Other people's kids seemed to be in tune with their surroundings.

I've seen these other children working in local gas stations, restaurants, and stores to earn their own spending money and college tuition.

What's that, Lord? Well, yes, I have heard news reports and statistics about teenage pregnancies, drug addiction, and suicides. I'm appalled at the number of robberies, murders, and rapes committed by teenagers. And all this time I've been worried about my children being lazy, sloppy, and disrespectful. I guess I should be thankful for the kids I've got.

Still, I wonder why these children sitting in front

of me are so good.

Oh-Oh! The little boy just grabbed the hymnal away from his sister, and she punched him in the side. The parents have intervened and are giving each other long-suffering looks. I'm positive I heard them mutter something about "other people's kids."

The sermon is over and I have no idea what it was about, but I think I have learned an important lesson this morning.

Thank You, Lord, for giving me normal children. Help me to quit expecting perfection and to appreciate them as they are. Keep me from coveting other people's kids.

> Bless the Lord, O my soul, and forget not all his benefits.
>
> Psalm 103:2

> I will pour my Spirit upon your descendants, and my blessing on your offspring.
>
> Isaiah 44:3b

Who Am I?

Where is my place, Lord?

For a long time I believed it was in my home. I felt strongly that my children needed me here, and indeed they did for many years. However, they seem quite indifferent to my presence now. If I call from work to talk to them, they are impatient for me to say what I have to say and hang up. They tell me I am interfering with their TV programs.

Still, I'm concerned about the lack of time I'm able to spend with my children. In my case the quality is affected by the quantity. The days are too short, and my life is too harried.

I have great difficulty understanding the simultaneous narrations they throw at me as soon as I come in the door. How do You do it, Lord? I don't understand how You can listen to millions of prayers, sort them out, and answer each of us individually.

There are never enough hours in a day to get everything done. All too often I take my frustrations out on the kids by snapping at them or being sarcastic.

You know I'd prefer to stay home, but our financial condition at the moment precludes any free choice. I'm not sure if my desire to stay home is for me or for them. I enjoy being able to run my home at a more leisurely pace, with time to pursue hobbies and visit friends.

My kids understand that my working makes that new pair of shoes or a pizza possible. That's probably why they don't object. They're a mercenary bunch. They even sacrifice some of their own time occasionally to cook supper or clean house.

I feel strongly that You led me to this particular job at this time. Nevertheless, the guilts surround me like wild dogs after their prey. Whether I go to work or stay home, they nip at my heels.

Many other women work outside the home and have their lives under control. Why do I find it so difficult?

Lord, I need longer days, more energy, and Your assurance that I am doing an adequate job as a mother.

Tell me who I am, Lord—a wife, mother, secretary, writer, or what?

Calm my shaky nerves and help me to accept my limitations. I cannot do and be everything to everyone. Assist me in setting up workable schedules, but make me flexible enough to abandon them when my children's needs are more important. I want to be a good mother even though I'm working. Show me how, Lord.

Let me never lose sight of my most important title, YOUR CHILD.

She looks well to the ways of her household, and does not eat the bread of idleness. Her children rise up and call her blessed; her husband also, and he praises her: "Many women have done excellently, but you surpass them all."

Proverbs 31:27-29

Put on the new nature, created after the likeness of God in true righteousness and holiness.

Ephesians 4:24

No Smoking, Please

Father, smoking cigarettes seems like one of the lesser evils that threaten our teenagers. Parents and kids alike sometimes fall into the trap of believing it's not harmful when compared to alcohol and pot.

Certainly our intellect knows better. We are confronted daily with evidence of the effects of tobacco, and we teach these facts to our children at school. So why don't they listen?

Is it because they see so many adults who seem unconcerned about the possible health hazards? I recently read in the paper that the number of people who smoke is increasing despite all the advertising against it.

It's difficult for young people who are in good physical shape to conceive of future illnesses caused by their present habits. We mothers begin worrying about their health long before they're born. We watch our eating habits carefully during the months we are pregnant and we monitor their diet throughout their childhood.

Then we arrive at these teen years when we must let them take control. Our well-meaning advice is taken as nagging.

Lord, let them believe and understand the voices of the experts and refrain from tainting their bodies with tobacco. You have blessed all my children with good health. I pray that they will continue to make intelligent choices and that You will give them the courage to resist any temptations that conflict with Your good sense.

Do you not know that your body is a temple of the Holy Spirit within you, which you have from God? You are not your own; you were bought with a price. So glorify God in your body.

1 Corinthians 6:19,20

Employment Enigma

Father, these kids have got to get jobs! It's the only solution to the conflict between their caviar tastes and our peanut-butter-and-jelly budget.

Besides, work develops responsibility, which in turn would give our children confidence in themselves, as well as their own spending money. Their father often reminds them that he does not have an endless supply of cash.

I hear a wide variety of excuses, Lord. They don't have time; they have too much homework; there aren't enough openings. I agree that washing dishes, making beds, pumping gas, or lighting smudge pots is not exactly a glamorous career, but at least there's a lot of room for advancement!

I admit that my own opinion is divided. I agree with all the reasons for them to gain employment. However, a part of me wants to tell them to enjoy life now while they're young because the time will soon be here when they must be serious about work.

Nevertheless we must all do what we have to do. Work is something we don't always enjoy; but if we wish to live in even a modest degree of comfort, we perform. I guess that's what self-discipline is all about—doing what we have to do even when we don't want to do it.

This is another one of those traits that my children must develop within themselves. I can't make them into responsible beings by forcing them to get jobs. My attempts to do so only cause them to be stubborn and defensive about the subject.

Take the blinders off their eyes, Lord, and let them see that life in the real world involves a mixture of hard work and pleasure. Let them see the doors of opportunity that You leave open for them, and let them understand that with Your support and a good attitude any job can be a good one.

The soul of the sluggard craves, and gets nothing, while the soul of the diligent is richly supplied.

Proverbs 13:4

Whatever your task, work heartily, as serving the Lord and not men.

Colossians 3:23

If anyone will not work, let him not eat. For we hear that some of you are living in idleness, mere busybodies, not doing any work. Now such persons we command and exhort in the Lord Jesus Christ to do their work in quietness and to earn their own living.

2 Thessalonians 3:10-12

Not Again!

O Lord, here they come again!

Another crop of gray hairs is about to appear on my head. My younger son and daughter are starting to drive.

My nerves had just begun to recover from the last four years of my older son's driving, and now I must replay the scenes. I'm not looking forward to speeding tickets, dented fenders, higher insurance rates, and empty gas tanks.

I'm a little more prepared this time, but that doesn't make it any easier. If the phone rings while one of my children has the car, I flinch. As I flash my husband a "What now?" look and race to the phone, I imagine the car breaking down, or worse yet—an accident. The unsuspecting party on the other end of the line is confused by my strangled, apprehensive "Hello?"

There are a few new problems this time around, since we have two young drivers and only one car. Also, these children must put up with more restrictions due to former expensive lessons and present financial stresses.

Gas, insurance, tires, etc. keep going up, and their chances for part-time employment are slim. "Can't they understand we're in the midst of a depression?" my husband asks.

In addition to all these irritating elements I have to put up with criticism of my own driving. You know how I dreaded telling them about my speeding ticket (the first one in 20 years, remember).

Give me strength, Lord, to get through the next

few years. Instill in my children good judgment and defensive driving skills.

Keep me from overreacting when I ride with them and help me to be fair in my decisions regarding their use of the car. Let me not presuppose their misbehavior because of past situations over which they had no control.

Trust in the Lord with all your heart, and do not rely on your insight.
                                     Proverbs: 3:5

The former things shall not be remembered or come into mind.
                                     Isaiah 65:17b

Do not be anxious about tomorrow, for tomorrow will be anxious for itself. Let the day's own trouble be sufficient for the day.

                           Matthew 6:34

Premature Parenting

Father, what would I do if my daughter became pregnant?

I'd rather not have to face that problem, and I'm hopeful I will not.

First I'd probably yell and cry awhile. Then I'd try to pull myself together and tell my daughter I love her. Despite any feelings of anger and disappointment I would never turn my child away. Instead, I'd try to help her decide what to do, and I'd support her.

I could not sanction an abortion unless my daughter's life were in danger. After holding three beautiful babies in my arms I could not deny the right of children to be born.

Neither could I force my daughter, or my sons, into a loveless marriage. If the young couple were insistent and committed to marrying I might concur, depending on their ages and mental maturity.

Many girls today are choosing to stay single and keep their babies. This sometimes lays a burden on society to help both the mother and child. If my daughter were faced with this decision I hope she would put the welfare of her baby first and honestly assess whether she could fulfill the responsibilities of motherhood.

I realize that giving up a child is a heart-rending sacrifice. Women and children who were separated are now attesting to the heartbreak they suffered and are seeking to bridge the years apart. Yet many would-be parents are waiting with love to pour out on an adopted child.

Since every girl and every situation is different, I would not presume to make any all-inclusive edicts.

Lord, I know You care deeply for young people who have made mistakes, and You can help them change their lives. All they have to do is ask.

Keep my daughter in your constant care. I pray that she would always let her love for You control her actions. I'm so glad she knows You. Having You for a friend enabled me to get through those years. I know it will enable her too.

Keep your heart with all vigilance, for from it flow the springs of life.

Proverbs 4:23

No temptation has overtaken you that is not common to man. God is faithful, and he will not let you be tempted beyond your strength, but with the temptation will also provide the way of escape, that you may be able to endure it.

1 Corinthians 10:13

Come now, let us reason together, says the Lord: though your sins be as scarlet, they shall be white as snow; though they are red like crimson, they shall become like wool.

Isaiah 1:18

Recyclable Relationships

Father, these stories about throwaway teenagers make me livid. What kind of people can throw their children out like yesterday's garbage?

I wept through a recent news special about this subject. It featured kids of the same ages as my sons and daughter who are living on the streets and resorting to any means at hand to secure money, food, and shelter. Some had fled from physical abuse, others from indifference. They expressed the feeling that nobody cared about them. I was indignant at the mother who received a message from her child through a runaway hotline, but left no answer.

I know I shouldn't make snap judgments about these parents without knowing their whole story. Some parents have reached a point where they can bear no more pain and conflict. It doesn't necessarily mean they have stopped loving. There are many others who are searching desperately for their children and long to receive word that the kids are okay. The volunteers who are trying to help said that most parents send back messages pleading for the kids to come back so they can work on the problems.

Lord, bless these people at hotlines and shelters who reunite families. Assist the parents and the children who are working to mend their broken relationships.

Keep my own family from reaching a point of confrontation where the children leave or are pushed out in anger. Let me never close the door or give up on my children. Keep my arms open as Yours are to always welcome the prodigal.

Let not loyalty and faithfulness forsake you; bind them about your neck, write them on the tablet of your heart.

Proverbs 3:3

Hidden Love

Why is it so hard, Lord, to show the love I feel for my children?

When they were young it was easy to reach out and hug them. Then they began to shrink away with, "Aw, Mom!" As I bent to kiss them goodnight they would cover their face with their blankets. Now they dodge my attempts to fix their collars or fluff their hair. Even an intent look is suspect.

"What's wrong?" they ask. "Why are you staring at me?"

My words don't help much. Instead of speaking praise and encouragement I communicate disapproval. It's no wonder they think I don't care about them.

Instead of "Good morning," I shout, "Get up! Hurry or you'll miss your bus!"

When my children come home I ask, "Where have you been? Why are you late?" before they even close the door. Without giving them a chance to answer I continue, "There's a lot of work to do, so get busy! Don't throw your coats there! I spend all day cleaning up after you!"

I want to be like the understanding TV mothers who greet their children with warm smiles, cookies and milk, and a cordial "It's nice to have you home. How was your day?" So much for my good intentions.

Since I don't excel at touching or speaking love, I try to express it with clean clothes and a hot meal, but they think these actions are required motherly duties rather than gifts of love.

Lord, let the love in my heart overflow into my words and deeds. Break down the barriers that surround my feelings, and free me to hug my children no matter what their ages may be.

I pray that they will always remember that I love them and You love them. If they forget everything else I've taught them but have confidence that they are loved, they can overcome any obstacle they may encounter. Love is a terrific bulldozer.

> "Love never ends; as for prophecies, they will pass away; as for tongues, they will cease; as for knowledge, it will pass away."
>
> 1 Corinthians 13:8

Make love your aim.

1 Corinthians 14:1

Above all these put on love, which binds everything together in perfect harmony.

Colossians 3:14

It's Been One of Those Days

Lord, You're the only One who'd ever believe what my day was like.

Pressed for time to finish the cookie jar that I planned as a gift, I took it to work and painted furiously during my lunch hour and coffee break. I was hopeful that I could complete my project by the following evening.

Then I received that call from Lana saying it was imperative that she have by tomorrow the dress I'd been working on. I tried to explain that I'm only a mortal with limited ability, but she kept on begging me to try.

As I drove home from work I commiserated with You over my dilemma. Although I did not want to disappoint my child, I wanted to go to Writer's Club and paint when I got home. My psychosense told me I should insist that she wear another dress, and that I fulfill my other commitments.

Then I walked into the house and found that the kitchen table had broken in two. (It was a direct result of somebody sitting in the middle of it.) Tim and Lana were hovering over the pieces, conferring on how to fix it.

Wasn't I cool and calm, Lord? I cooked a stand-up hamburger dinner and left for my meeting. When I came home I was astonished to find that the children had actually fixed the table themselves. Forgive my lack of faith in their work, but I have visions of the table collapsing on our laps while we're eating dinner one night.

Now it's 2:30 in the morning. The dress is finished; the cookie jar is not. I'll have to take it to
work again. How will I ever get it done by tonight?

I know; I know; the modern woman does not let
her children manipulate her. There's no good
reason why she couldn't wear another dress. I
don't have to kill myself trying to be the perfect
mother.

So why did I do it, Lord?

You know, don't you?

Because love is a hard habit to break.

Let us not grow weary in well-doing, for in due
season we shall reap, if we do not lose heart.

Galatians 6:9

Not My Kids!

Heavenly Father, one of the major fears we parents have today is that our children will use drugs to dull their emotional aches.

We all want to believe this problem won't touch our families. Yet statistics show that a large percentage of teenagers are smoking marijuana and taking other drugs. Many of these kids are from middle-class Christian families in which parents have devoted much time, money, and love to their children.

Nothing prepares us for that dreaded moment when we find a bong, a pipe, or a baggie of dried green weed in our son's or daughter's coat pocket or dresser drawer.

"Why?" we ask ourselves. "How could this happen?" We heap guilt and blame upon ourselves, feeling that we have failed as parents and as Christians.

Who can we talk to, Lord? We don't want our pastors or Christian friends to know our shameful secrets. *Their* children seem so perfect.

Psychologists suggest that we talk to our children about our feelings without overreacting or trying to force our opinions on them. We're supposed to leave the decision to them. I can't accept that, Lord. How can a parent watch a child destroy himself and keep silent? We may not be able to make them accept our advice, but we can't quit trying.

On the other hand, some so-called experts insist that we should put our feet down and give our children the choice of giving up their bad habits or leaving home. That might work in some instances, but what happens if the kids go? You can't communicate with an empty chair. Furthermore, the city streets are littered with young people who can't or won't go home.

Help us all to find the answers. Guide and direct us and our children to follow Your will for our lives and to avoid the lures of social acceptability.

Give us the courage to drop the "good Christian" masks we wear and be honest with each other. How else can we uphold and comfort others who are hurting?

If we in any way have caused our children to turn to marijuana to feel good, forgive us, Lord. Free us from the guilt that clouds our perception and help us to keep the door of love open, always.

Release our children from harmful desires and protect them from the deceiver.

We can bear the burdens and find the solutions, Lord, with Your assistance.

Wait for the Lord; be strong, and let your heart take courage; yea, wait for the Lord!

Psalm 27:14

This is the confidence which we have in him, that if we ask anything according to his will he hears us. And if we know that he hears us in whatever we ask, we know that we have obtained the requests made of him.

1 John 5:14,15

Housekeeper's Lament

Tell me, Lord: What's a mother to do?

This house is becoming a serious health hazard. I expect to find a "C" rating from the Board of Health posted on the door any day now.

How can I change this family of slobs?

When the children were young enough to be afraid of my anger I could get them to clean their rooms regularly. Then they discovered that I really wasn't so tough, and they began placating me with "I'll do it later, Mom." I alternately used threats and bribes, and I threw fits in order to force these kids into neatness.

I know my inconsistency hasn't helped. One day I go on a rampage screaming and nagging, and the next day I give up and decide to let them live like pigs if that's what they want.

Whenever I seek answers from books or psychologists I find a different opinion. As a parent and owner of the house I have the right to insist on clean bedrooms, but on the other hand I should decide if they're important.

Now I grit my teeth and shut their doors, refusing to enter even to pick up their dirty clothes. There have been some results. The kids have been putting their clothes into the laundry chute or suffering the consequences and washing their own clothes.

It wouldn't be so bad if their messes stayed confined to their bedrooms, but this clutter all over the living room drives me crazy. As I look around me now I see Coke bottles, glasses, books, book bags, shoes, coats, and a calculator.

Oops, I also see *my* coat, shoes, ceramics I've been painting, etc. Do you suppose my children have inherited their sloppiness from me?

Oh, well, I probably wouldn't want to live in a showcase anyway. This room would be morbidly empty without my husband reading and scattering newspapers about or my children sitting on the floor or couch doing their homework surrounded by their books, papers, and snacks.

Thank You, Lord, for these people who clutter up my house and my life.

> . . . always and for everything giving thanks in the name of our Lord Jesus Christ to God the father.
>
> Ephesians 5:20

Curfew Confusion

Lord, what's a reasonable curfew?

My children challenge, stretch, or ignore whatever time I set. Our ideas of time are a long way from coinciding.

"You just don't want me to have any fun!" my son accused.

"What time do your friends have to be home?" I once asked.

The answer was that other kids are not required to meet any deadlines, but amble home whenever they feel like it.

My research on this subject revealed contrary information. The other parents I talked to were involved in the same "nobody else does" game.

Lord, You know I want my children to enjoy these special years, but I need to get some sleep at night, and I can't close my eyes until my chicks are all home. Am I being selfish?

The fight with my oldest finally ended when I lifted his curfew. Now that he has all that freedom he comes home earlier than the curfew times I had imposed on him. Kids! Who can figure them out?

My other children have not yet begun to strain at the leash. I pray that You will give signals to let me know when to hold tight and when to let go.

And don't let me forget that five-dollar bet with my son. He insists he will never tell his kids when they have to come home. This I have to see! Forgive me, Lord, but I want to be around to say, "I told you so."

The Lord will keep your going out and your coming in from this time forth and for evermore.

Psalm 121:8

The mind of all the rash will have good judgment.

Isaiah 32:4

This Silence Is Deafening

Listen to the silence, Lord.

Isn't it beautiful? It's a rare phenomenon in this house. I can hardly believe my ears!

My children are all out for the evening, and my husband is out of town. I relish this solitude. I can read my new book without interruption.

Hmm, this book just doesn't hold my attention. I'll work on my manuscripts instead.

Something's missing, Lord. My thoughts are fragmented. I'm grinding out words that don't fit together.

This house is like a morgue! Who can write in such an atmosphere? I'll just flick on some music and the TV set.

There, that's better, but not quite perfect. I know what's lacking—it's the absence of bodies.

I've been writing articles in the middle of the living-room floor with the TV on and sounds of Tim's TV and Lana's stereo in the background. Now that I've got the quiet I've been praying for, my mind has suddenly gone blank.

Help me to adjust to being alone. Soon my children will be gone, and I must tolerate the quiet times as I have learned to put up with the noise.

I look forward to this change in my lifestyle, but dread it at the same time.

For now, I'll just turn the volume up a little and try to get some work done.

I will not leave you desolate; I will come to you.

John 14:18

He makes me lie down in green pastures.
He leads me beside still waters; he restores my soul.

Psalm 23:2,3a

I Believe In
Young People

Father, I do a lot of griping about kids, but I don't believe they're hopeless.

I hate to hear people grouping kids all together and saying, "All kids today are alike. They don't want to read or learn. They have no goals and aren't interested in anything constructive."

When I watch children in concerts, athletic events, or recitals I get a lump in my throat. It doesn't necessarily have to be something my own kids are involved in. Anytime kids exhibit the dedication required to perform well, I get all teary-eyed.

Lord, help us to recognize that a few bad kids do not taint the whole generation. We need to remember our own teenage years and understand the pain and frustrations these kids have.

Yes, today's children *are* different from their predecessors. They challenge and question the information they are given. Isn't that what we've taught them to do? We've pushed them to explore new ideas, but we're frightened when they reject our lifestyles. Perhaps they see too many adults who drift aimlessly through life or whose commitments bring them no joy. Is it any wonder they're confused?

Keep me from being too quick to criticize and too slow to priase the children I come in contact with.

Father, help me to be a good example for my children and their friends. Let them see that my commitment to You has given my life substance.

Since I trust You to guide them, Lord, I have no fears of leaving the future in their hands.

> Show yourself in all respects a model of good deeds, and in your teaching show integrity, gravity, and sound speech that cannot be censured, so that an opponent may be put to shame, having nothing evil to say of us.
>
> Titus 2:7,8

> Let no one despise your youth, but set the believers an example in speech and conduct, in love, in faith, in purity.
>
> 1 Timothy 4:12

They Make Me Feel So Dumb

Help, Lord!

This homework is getting harder each year. I think there's a conspiracy afoot by the educational system to show us parents up. (Or else they're trying to insure that the kids do their own homework!)

I got A's in algebra, but this modern math is baffling. Now that Tim is taking precalculus he has left me way behind.

The questions Tim asks me while he's studying his physics boggle my mind. Lord, I really don't care what the average accelerated speed of a revolving disc moving across a revolving circle is.

A few years ago when the kids began asking questions I could not answer I saved face by telling them to look it up. "You'll never learn if I just tell you," I said. They soon figured out that I was actually saying, "I don't know."

"Mom, when I was little I thought you knew everything," Tim once said. What a blow when our children discover our limitations!

Now I tell my children my education is not yet complete. I've just learned different things first.

They still seek the knowledge of their father and me in regard to some aspects of life. We're apparently not entirely obsolete.

It's good to be needed and to have some of our wisdom affirmed.

I just praise and thank You for Your endless store of knowledge which You allow us to draw on. Our

need for You will never end.
I admit I don't know it all, Lord; teach me the rest.

The Lord gives wisdom; from his mouth come knowledge and understanding.

Proverbs 2:6

Keep hold of instruction, do not let go; guard her, for she is your life.

Proverbs 4:13

The Accident

Where were You, Lord?

How could my child be involved in an accident when I cover him daily with prayers for his protection?

I had often half-expected that phone call, but I was unprepared for it when it came.

"Let me talk to Dad," my son said.

"Why?" I asked.

"Just let me talk to Dad."

He seemed to know instinctively that his father's first reaction would be to deal with the necessary practicalities.

Although I talked a lot about relying on You, I initially fell apart. Some example I set! Later I realized how fortunate we were to have just lost a car and not a son.

We have seen a repeat of this scenario several times. My poor little car is battered and bruised, but my son is still in one piece. Each time he has learned a new lesson and has become a little more cautious in his driving.

Many families are not as lucky as we have been. I don't understand why, but I know it is not Your will that these young people be killed or seriously injured. I have seen You at work comforting the survivors and giving encouragement and healing to the victims.

Still, I release my children to You, Lord. When they enter any vehicle, I pray that You would be at their sides. Knowing that You are with them calms my fears. I am confident that no matter what may happen to them, Your love will never leave them.

I lift praises to You and thanks that Your love is no accident.

Fear not, therefore; you are of more value than many sparrows.

Matthew 10:31

When I am afraid, I put my trust in thee. In God, whose word I praise, in God I trust without a fear. What can flesh do to me?

Psalm 56:3,4

Ineffective Anesthesia

Father, they say the number-one cause of death for teenagers is the combination of alcohol and automobiles. What can we do about it?

Our laws against minors' possession of alcóhol haven't retarded its use by teenagers. In fact some states have relaxed their laws in order to allow the older teens to drink legally.

Lord, far too many families are suffering because of a member's drinking habit. An alcoholic's self-inflicted pain hurts everyone around him. Many alcoholics confess that their problem began as teenage social drinking.

I realize that this problem is not new to You. Your prophets and apostles admonished others against misusing wine thousands of years ago.

Today drinking is a widespread socially acceptable pastime. TV programs, magazines, and movies depict cocktails as the way to unwind and a drink during a crisis as a talisman for courage or an anesthetic for life's blows. Celebrations and fun are portrayed as synonymous with drinking liquor.

It's difficult for us parents to refute these pictures, Lord. How can we keep our kids from falling victim to this alluring addiction? Even when we get our message across, our kids still believe that none of the tragic consequences of the use of alcohol will touch *them*.

"Don't worry, Mom. I can handle it," they say.

Lord, help our children to love themselves enough to want to keep their bodies in good health —free from the harmful effects of alcohol. Help

them to find Your healing antidotes for their growing pains, and to turn away from temporary cover-
ups. I pray that they will reject the enticements of
social drinking that surround them before some
calamitous event forces their understanding.

As for those who have already made the right
choices, uphold them, Lord. Keep them from faltering in the face of peer pressure. Strengthen their
resolve.

May they all soon know You are the perfect
painkiller and that You offer a "high" that fills all
the morning-afters with joy.

> Who has woe? Who has sorrow? Who has
> strife? Who has complaining? Who has
> redness of eyes? Those who tarry long over
> wine, who go to try mixed wine. Do not look
> at wine when it is red, when it sparkles in the
> cup and goes down smoothly. At the last it
> bites like a serpent, and stings like an adder.
> Your eyes will see strange things, and your
> mind utter perverse things. You will be like
> one who lies down in the midst of a sea, like
> one who lies on the top of a mast. "They
> struck me," you will say, "but I was not hurt;
> they beat me, but I did not feel it. When shall I
> awake? I wll seek another drink."
>
> Proverbs 23:29-35

Thicker Than Blood

Lord, at this stage of their lives our children consider their friendships to be more important than their family relationships.

My teenagers claim that their friends understand them but that their father and I do not. Ouch! That hurts, Lord!

I think their friends are often undeserving of my children's loyalty. I have felt the disappointments that my children suffer when they are left out or put down. I am angry when my kids are hurt. I know I can't protect them from these pains, since they're part of the natural process of growing up.

Also, I'm afraid, Lord, that their friends will cause them to change their values. I used to think that if we built a good foundation our children could not put any defective structures on top of it. However, kids in their teens are more concerned about the opinions of their peers than those of their parents. They sometimes put their own consciences aside in order to fit in with the crowd.

It is for these reasons that we parents want to choose our children's friends. We long to protect them from damaging associations.

Although our motives are good, our own judgment is not always correct. Making character judgments is extremely difficult. Our insight is so limited. A child whom we see as polite and well-behaved may be entirely different in the company of his peers. We may perceive a child who is quiet and uncomfortable around adults as being a "hood" when he actually is a good kid but is extremely shy.

Attempts to impart our sage advice about friends to our teenagers are met with indignation. I can remember my own reactions if my parents criticized my friends. I was fiercely loyal to anyone they didn't approve of and incensed that they made conclusions from outskirt observations. Now I can see how difficult it is to do otherwise.

If I could I would wave a magic wand over my children's peer relationships. I would endow them with friends who have high moral standards and who would never inflict any emotional wounds on my kids.

I hear Your voice within me saying, "No!" I cannot save my children from the pains of friendships without denying them the joys. Neither can I insulate them from making some bad choices and suffering the consequences. Experience is a better teacher than I. In time they will find out for themselves who is really a friend and who is not.

Lord, please guide my children toward wholesome, healthy peer relationships. Stand with them when they must stand apart from the crowd in order to follow Your will.

Thank You for Your perfect friendship.

There are friends who pretend to be friends, but there is a friend who sticks closer than a brother.

Proverbs 18:24

Greater love has no man than this, that a man lay down his life for his friends.

John 15:13

Accelerated Living

Help, Lord!

I long for a quiet, restful place where I can escape the sounds of twangy electric guitars, ringing telephones, and these high-powered units of energy that I call my children.

Here I am in the midst of continuous chaos, fixing short-order meals and arranging rides for dancing lessons or band practice.

Whatever happened to long, leisurely family dinners and placid evenings in front of a warm, crackling fire? Do such pictures of domestic tranquility actually exist, or are they only mirages?

I wonder what would happen if everything came to a complete stop and we were all trapped in the house together, with no electricity or phones, and none of our vehicles worked. Could we carry on a real family discussion? It's been a long time since we've had time to speak in paragraphs instead of sentence fragments.

I wish we could all rearrange our schedules so we could have a few hours to just talk or enjoy some activity together. Yes, Lord, I know it would be difficult. At this stage of life my children think of family togetherness as a hangman's noose around their necks—pure torture.

Ah, well, I can dream, can't I? Meanwhile I have to cut this short and pick up Lana from basketball practice, stop at the store for milk, and get supper over with so I can get to my class.

I feel like a racehorse in the backstretch running toward a finish line that keeps moving further and further away. What do You think, Lord? Will I make it? I hope there's a lush, green meadow where I can collapse when I get to the end of this race and find solace for my jangled nerves.

A tranquil mind gives life to the flesh.

Proverbs 14:30

Thou dost keep him in perfect peace whose mind is stayed on thee.

Isaiah 26:3

You were wearied with the length of your way, but you did not say, "It is hopeless"; you found new life for your strength, and so you were not faint.

Isaiah 57:10

In a Manner of Speaking

Father, is it too much to expect my children to use good manners here at home?

All I ask is to be spoken to politely. A little "Please" here or a "Thank you" there would do a lot to brighten my day.

Haven't I used these words often when speaking to my children? Why don't they pick up some of my good habits instead of imitating my faults?

"Just empty words," they claim.

"Saying 'I'm sorry' doesn't help anything. What does 'Excuse me' mean? Why do you ask if I'll do it 'please' when I don't have a choice?"

Why can't they understand that these traditional phrases, boring as they may be, signify concern about someone else's feelings?

Young people often cry that they want to be treated with respect, but they are stingy about giving it out.

Lord, these children are not always insensitive clouts. Reports from their teachers and my friends indicate that my children often respond to other people with exceptional politeness.

But at home their behavior shows little existence of good manners. Is it because they just don't care about the feelings of the family members, or because they expect us to overlook their rudeness because we love them? They are so wrapped up in themselves that they barely recognize that the rest of the family exists, unless they need something from us. Then they turn on the charm.

Knowing that this is a common characteristic in teenagers doesn't make it any easier to bear.

Lord, I'm sorry that I sometimes act the same way toward You. The fact that You love me even though I am an ingrate inspires me to make my life a Thank You.

> Let your speech always be gracious, seasoned with salt, so that you may know how you ought to answer everyone.
>
> Colossians 4:6

An Angry Martyr

Lord, there are times when I really don't like my family.

I'm tired of their constant demands and their lack of consideration for me. They expect too much!

From the minute I walk in the door after work, I hear,

"What's for supper? When will it be ready?"

"You have to help me with my history!"

"Can you take me to the store? I need notebook paper (or nylons, or face cleanser)."

Besides all these regular requests of my time, they always expect me to bake, decorate, and be prepared for the holidays and special events. Just once in my life I'd like to hear, "We'll fix supper and clean up if you want to write or just relax."

I was fuming tonight as I cleaned up the kitchen (alone, naturally—they all had too much homework). Isn't anyone ever going to recognize that I need help too?

Ordinarily I enjoy being needed, but with the pressure of deadlines facing me I just wish they'd all leave me alone. I feel used. They utilize our money, our food, our car, and our time, and yet they're annoyed when we ask a favor in return.

That's what we're here for, though, isn't it? If we were not used by the people we love, we would deteriorate from neglect.

Help me, Father, to forgive and to let go of my resentment now, before I go to bed.

Thank You for allowing me to use You, Lord. Thank You for always listening to my pleas for help.

Good sense makes a man slow to anger, and it is his glory to overlook an offense.

Proverbs 19:11

What to Do?
What to Do?

Lord, Tim is apprehensive about his future after he graduates from high school this year. He thinks he wants to go to college, but he is not confident of his academic abilities even though his grades have always been above average. He's bewildered about what course of study to follow and has been unable to choose a career. He doesn't know if he should live in the dorm or commute. I could go on for hours listing the decisions he's worrying about.

They're all important questions, and they need to be answered soon, but I'm concerned that his anxiety is excessive. I tell him to relax, but of course it does no good. He thinks I don't understand. I can't seem to convince him that none of these decisions would be irrevocable.

You'd think that after watching his dad and me fumble through life, changing our minds at every corner, he'd understand that few things in life are final. Even if we choose unwisely we can go back to square one and begin again.

He's afraid of failure. He wants definite answers and a mapped-out course to success and happiness, which is practically impossible.

Lord, I feel the most important decision he has to make is whether to accept Your love and take You on as his Navigator. Then no matter what flight plan he chooses he'll arrive at his destination safely.

I have made many ill-advised choices in my life, but You always help me to stay in orbit.

Stay with my son, Lord. Bring peace to his worried mind and give him the ability to control his life with confidence. Keep me from forcing my opinions upon him. Just as I let him stumble when he was learning to walk, I must allow him to make a few poor decisions in order to help him grow wiser. You have not made me Your puppet; I'll not make him mine.

A man's mind plans his way, but the Lord directs his steps.
Proverbs 16:9

All the paths of the Lord are steadfast love and faithfulness.
Psalm 25:10

The Dating Dilemma

Lord, I know parents who set up strict rules governing their children's dating habits. They draw up timetables that connect their children's ages to specific kinds of dates—mixed unpaired groups, double dates, single pairs, and car dates. Permissible time limits and destinations are also outlined beforehand. Ideally this approach should result in a conflict-free relationship in this one area between parents and children.

However, the best of theories often evaporate in the real world of parenting teenagers. I've seen disastrous results when the rules are too rigid and also when there are no set policies.

Teenagers do not take kindly to any suggestions that they are not able to make good character assessments. I can remember being instinctively drawn to anyone my father disapproved of. Overly strict parents often obtain a result that is quite different from the one they are striving for.

The no-limit approach has similar consequences. Kids who are not bound by rules do as they please and sometimes question whether their parents care what they do.

At times like these it pays to be a middle-of-the-roader.

My children have been slower than most at the dating game, and I'm not anxious to have them move any faster.

Because the days of chaperoned dates and arranged marriages are over, all parents can do is to hope and pray that we have imparted some degree of perceptiveness to our children regarding people, relationships, and environments.

Give me the wisdom to know how to advise my children in their friendships with the opposite sex without making them feel we don't trust them. Show me how to give my children enough freedom to make their own decisions about dates and partners and to pull in the reins when they need my protection. Bolster their sagging self-images so that their relations with other people will be based on intelligent and honest discernment.

My son, if your heart is wise, my heart too will be glad.

Proverbs 23:15

It is my prayer that your love may abound more and more, with knowledge and all discernment, so that you may approve what is excellent, and may be pure and blameless for the day of Christ, filled with the fruits of righteousness which come through Jesus Christ, to the glory and praise of God.

Philippians 1:9-11

This Is Music?

Lord, I've always been open to all kinds of music, but I can't take these high-pitched vibrations. The discordant sounds that fill the air when my son is home have an adverse effect on my temperament. These strains will never "soothe the savage beast."

The noise level is enough to drive any sane person crazy. It rises with the voices of the other members of the family yelling, "Turn it down!" and an increase in volume of the TV so it can be heard.

When I enter my son's room to give him our message, I find him as close to his stereo as he can get, listening intently. He gives me a "Parents are impossible!" look as I turn down the volume and deliver a lecture on what he's doing to his hearing.

"It's not loud," he insists.

I know better, but I still explain that the house is expanding and pulsating with each beat like a bull-frog's throat, and couldn't he be a little more concerned about the rest of us?

I realize I am being somewhat hypocritical. If he were playing music I liked I probably wouldn't mind the volume, but I prefer that his electronic twangs be turned down to a whisper.

With all his musical ability and talent I expect him to have better taste. There I go sounding like a member of the older generation. When I was a teenager I was infuriated by adults' attacks on my favorite rock-and-roll idols and music. Now I'm playing critic.

I do enjoy some pop (at an extremely low volume), country, gospel, easy listening, and light classical. All my children pass judgment on my taste also.

Sometimes I wonder if it was a mistake to let my son saturate his brain with rock music. When he was into mostly hard rock it seemed to change his personality. I can see a gradual recovery as he has turned toward softer rock and jazz. I have even found myself liking some of his newer records.

It's so hard, Lord, to know what to do. Some parents bar rock music from their house and forbid the kids to go to concerts in an attempt to protect them. They consider it a parent's duty to firmly control their children's behavior. I agree and I disagree. I'm confused.

Forbidden fruit often has a strong, magnetic pull for teenagers. Perhaps if we make sure their musical diets are supplemented with some good-quality harmonious vitamins they will sort out the delicacies and throw away the garbage.

Guide my children and me, Lord, toward music which glorifies You.

> All things are lawful, but not all things are helpful. All things are lawful, but not all things build up.
>
> 1 Corinthians 10:23

> The wisdom from above is first pure, then peaceable, gentle, open to reason, full of mercy and good fruits, without uncertainty or insincerity.
>
> James 3:17

Tender Hearts

Father, I have not yet grown so old that I cannot remember what it was like to be young and in love.

I wish I could guarantee that my children would experience only the good feelings and never know the pain. They can't be separated, though, can they, Lord? Unless we remain vulnerable and open to hurt we cannot receive the love.

Remember how just passing that certain person in the school hallway and being smiled at or spoken to could put me on a cloud? Time seemed suspended when I was out with a boy I liked a lot and sleep was sweet when I dreamed about him. But the dreams ended when the relationship became too quarrelsome or distant, and there would be lonely nights spent waiting for the phone to ring. I'd like to spare my children those feelings of rejection.

Viewing the process from my position as a parent isn't any easier than it was while being the teen. Besides the empathy I feel for the kids, these situations evoke memories of my own painful involvements.

It's helpful for us parents to remember that our own broken hearts always managed to heal before we found another person to give it to. Looking back from this point, I'm grateful that I was not stuck with some of the boys I dated. My children do not appreciate my telling them that they will get over one love and find another. They view my sage advice as an attempt to run their lives.

What can I do, Lord? I can try to give them the

benefit of my experiences, but I can't force them to listen. Once again I rely on You to see that good sense prevails over emotion.

Also, I can be available for them whenever they want to talk, just as You are always there for me.

> Oh send out thy light and thy truth; let them lead me.
>
> Psalm 43:3

Therefore be imitators of God, as beloved children, and walk in love, as Christ loved us.

> Ephesians 5:1

On the Other Path

Father, my heart goes out to the parents of children in trouble.

There is a part of us that always feels responsible when our children err. We wonder what we did wrong and if it's too late to correct our mistakes.

It would be nice if our babies were delivered with lifetime warranties attached. Then if they didn't perform properly we could trade them in for a more efficient model. I'm just joking, Lord—I think.

A whole range of social services is available now for the child who has been caught doing something wrong by the police or school authorities. Through counseling, alternative education programs, and job opportunities, some children learn to make peace with and even become part of society. However, others remain at war with themselves and anyone they come in contact with.

Parents suffer long and silently and remain bewildered and guilt-ridden over the sins of their children. Christians are often hit harder than other parents because they have higher expectations. These things aren't supposed to happen to us—not to God-fearing, upright people who take their children to church every week and diligently teach them right from wrong. We are confused, hurt, and angry. How dare our kids choose the wrong path! They must do these things intentionally to hurt us.

The few instances when my own kids have been in trouble are miniscule when compared to the crimes that are committed daily by other young people. I'm sure these other parents would be scornful of my concern over tardiness, failing grades, or rebellion against authority. Yet my feelings of failure are no less than theirs. Now I understand how You suffer when we ignore Your teachings and choose paths that lead to destruction.

Bear us up, Lord. Enable us to stop playing Your part by taking the responsibility for all their actions and beating ourselves emotionally for their sins. Your Son has already paid the price for their mistakes and ours. Help us to accept the release from guilt that He offers.

Showering wayward kids with love is not an easy feat, Lord. We need to be filled with Your special brand of love in order to succeed.

The Lord waits to be gracious to you . . . he exalts himself to show mercy to you.

Isaiah 30:18

Consider him who endured from sinners such hostility against himself, so you may not grow weary or fainthearted. In your struggle against sin you have not yet resisted to the point of shedding your blood.

Hebrews 12:3,4

Endangered Species

Lord, must I apologize for staying married?

There are times when I feel I'm expected to. After all, I'm depriving my children of dual holidays and birthdays. Their wardrobes are limited by having only one set of contributing parents, and they have no alternate home to use as a threat.

I don't mean to be flip about this rampant epidemic called divorce, but I feel like an endangered species after being married 22 years.

It hasn't been an easy feat. Without Your daily presence it would be impossible. Like most couples, my husband and I have ups and downs, and I admit that during the down periods there's a temptation to give up. However, to do so would mean sacrificing the blessings of the good times.

I feel deeply for the children of broken marriages, since I have been in their shoes. While classes in "creative" separations and family therapy help may erase the hurts, some scars always remain.

I'm not passing judgment on those who can't make it. No one on the outside of a marriage can know the depths of pain some people are enduring or how much they can take. I know You are suffering with them and You forgive them when they are unable to find a substitute for divorce.

I do wonder, though, what would happen if we spent more time and effort on keeping our families together. Perhaps the divorce rate would diminish. It would for certain if we'd make You an intimate member of our family as You have made us part of Yours.

Our teenagers put added pressures on our husband-wife relationships, intentionally and unintentionally. The majority of arguments in our family the last few years have been over the kids. I have known few couples who agree on all facets of parenting teenagers. No doubt some balance is good for the kids, but it sure is hard on us, Lord.

I've been trying to impress upon my children that marriage is not a "happily-ever-after" affair and that love is more than romance. I feel that one of the major reasons for the failures is that we place too many expectations on each other. When we don't live up to each other's ideals we "fall out of love."

Lord, You have continued to love me for the last 40 years even though I am not always worthy of Your love, except through Jesus Christ. I can do no less for my husband and my children.

Cover our family with Your grace, and help us to never give up on each other.

Heal the hearts of those families who have suffered from divorce. Let them never feel estranged from Your love.

Beloved, let us love one another; for love is of God, and he who loves is born of God and knows God.

1 John 4:7

S-e-x

Lord, sexuality is really not my subject!

Why can't You just zap our children with instant knowledge of this topic and save parents of the inhibited generation a lot of anguish?

I've tried to be open, truthful, and unabashed whenever I discuss the subject with my children. I didn't even laugh when Gene (then in fifth grade) first asked me if sex was funny.

Here it is, I thought. We sat down and went over the basic information.

"Oh," he said when I had finished my lecture. "A kid at camp told me that, and I didn't believe him."

Years later, after he'd gone through classes in school (which I supplemented with Christian views), he informed me that sex is different today. Then I began to wonder if I'd missed something.

As the kids grew older, their questions ceased and they seemed uncomfortable when talking to me about sex. After I attended a class for parents on teaching sexuality to our children I shared the information with my kids and learned a lot about their attitudes.

I am upset with the assumption that all teenagers are or will be sexually active. You'd think my children were abnormal because they've been slow in starting to date.

I'm trying to be an enlightened parent, but I cannot deny my own feelings when it comes to teenage sexual involvements. I feel it is my duty to temper the present worldly view with what I consider to be Your will.

Lord, I'm in dire need of Your help here. Inspire me with answers that will not burden these children with guilt about sexual feelings, but at the same time will help them understand the responsibilities that an intimate relationship would involve and the possible consequences of their decisions. I know they can't just pretend that these feelings don't exist. After all, they are confronted daily with music, advertising, and literature that exploits these feelings.

Help me to supply accurate facts and present my opinions in an understandable way. Make sure my opinions coincide with Yours. Give me strength to hope that some of what I've said to them will filter into their brains. When I've done all I can, I give it to You and ask You to do the rest.

> Make me to know thy ways, O lord; teach me thy paths. Lead me in the truth, and teach me, for thou art the God of my salvation; for thee I wait all the day long.
>
> Psalm 25:4,5

> Can a man carry fire in his bosom and his clothes not be burned? Or can one walk upon hot coals and his feet not be scorched?
>
> Proverbs 6:27,28

> You were bought with a price. So glorify God in your body.
>
> 1 Corinthians 6:20

Dinner for Two

C'mon, Lord, this isn't fair!

I spent most of the day preparing a special supper. I'd been feeling guilty about the quick throw-together meals I'd been serving, and so I decided to cook a nutritious feast. I planned my whole day around a timetable for creating each course.

As I began to put the food on the table and call everyone to come, I was stabbed by these responses:

"What's that? Yuk, I'm not eating it! I'll make myself a couple hot dogs in the microwave."

"Mom, I don't have time to eat. I have to be at the school in 15 minutes. I'll grab a hamburger after practice. Got any money?"

"I'm not eating. You know I'm dieting."

There I stood in the middle of the kitchen, wondering whether to scream, cry, or threaten suicide if they didn't eat my dinner.

Thank You for answering my prayer for sanity. I thought for a moment I was going to freak out and throw the food at them. We both know how senseless that would have been, since I'm the one who would have had to clean it up.

Now, as my husband and I sit down to eat a meal that was intended for five people, I just ask You to free my digestive system of any repressed anger so I can enjoy this terrific supper.

I would feed you with the finest of the wheat,
and with honey from the rock I would satisfy
you.

Psalm 81:16

Let no evil talk come out of your mouths, but
only such as good for edifying, as fits the occasion, that it may import grace to those who
hear.

Ephesians 4:29

Listening to the Answers

Father, I owe You a huge apology.

Day after day I kneel before You with complaints and petitions. I close my eyes and bow my head, but then I forget to open my eyes and recognize Your answers.

I asked for patience, and You gave me children. I asked for wisdom, and You gave me children. I asked for understanding, and You gave me children.

You have walked beside me for 21 years while I have laughed, cried, worried, questioned, and agonized over this process of mothering. I doubt that I have ever expressed how grateful I am that You've been here. I know I never could have made it without You.

There have been times when I forgot to ask for Your help or doubted that You were listening. Lately I have come to see some of the solutions You have arranged behind the scenes.

I recall that afernoon when Gene took his sister to the bank and they were involved in a small accident on the way back to our shop. I sat at my desk with my head in my hands muttering, "Why? Why? Why?" and insisting that I couldn't take any more. No one will ever convince me that it was pure chance that a lady called to tell me there was a place for me in the Bible study that I'd signed up for a few weeks earlier. How did my name move so quickly to the top of the waiting list? Wasn't it because You knew my desperate need?

I see You at work in my husband and son's relationship, also. It may not be perfect yet, but it's much better than it was a few years ago.

Also, my oldest son is daily gaining in common sense, and slowly recognizing that his father and I do know a few things. I can hardly believe my ears when he asks for the advice he used to say he didn't want to hear.

You've helped me to understand and accept my other son's outbursts of rage as his release from being so introverted and controlled outside our home. Instead of blowing up myself, I am trying to build up his faltering self-image.

As my sons are naturally moving away from me both physically and emotionally, You are bringing my daughter closer. Although she's at an age when people have told me she would be a worse problem than the boys, we genuinely enjoy each other's company. Her personality reflects the fruits of Your Spirit within her.

What more can I say, Lord? I'm sorry for my whining and my neglect to express my love and gratitude to You.

Heal me of my blindness and my deafness, and open my mouth to sing praises.

Help me to tell other mothers who are fumbling in despair to have faith. You are there poking holes in the darkness and will guide them into daylight.

I will give thanks to the Lord with my whole heart.

Psalm 9:1

O Lord, open thou my lips, and my mouth shall show forth thy praise.

Psalm 51:15

Blessed be the Lord, who daily bears us up;
God is our salvation.

Psalm 68:19

The Halls of Knowledge

Lord, I have no right to complain about my children's schools and teachers if I neglect to hold them up to You in prayer.

I'm grateful that there are still educators who genuinely care about their students and don't just regard their position as a job. I have no sympathy for those who gripe about being baby-sitters. People become what they think they are.

My children's school years have been sprinkled with some exceptional instructors who have not only made contributions to my kids' intellects, but to their self-images as well. They inspire their students to perfect their talents and to study for knowledge rather than grades.

There are others who demand a lot from their students and are disliked for their efforts. Several years from now the kids will draw on the facts these teachers insisted they learn.

There are also some who tear down what the others have built by practicing extreme favoritism, by trying too hard to be one of the kids, or by being indifferent. I get annoyed when teachers try to make our children think as they do or when their rules are so inflexible that the students are no longer individuals.

Lord, I pray that You would direct my children toward the good teachers and negate the harmful effects of the mediocre ones.

Remind me to do what I can to correct the problems I observe by exercising my vote and being aware of what's going on. Also, remind me to express my thanks to the good teachers to encourage them to keep up the good work.

I realize that teachers, like parents, are only human, and that spending all that time cooped up with 30 kids hour after hour is bound to have an effect. Protect their sanity, Lord.

If the work which any man has built on the foundation survives, he will receive a reward.

1 Corinthians 3:14

Keep hold of instruction, do not let go; guard her, for she is your life.

Proverbs 4:13

Let not many of you become teachers, my brethren, for you know that we who teach shall be judged with greater strictness.

James 3:1

Modeling

Lord, there are times when my actions contradict my preaching.

For instance, yesterday I chided Lana for speaking ill of a girl she considers a "supersnob." Then I found myself talking about an acquaintance in a patronizing, self-righteous manner.

I tell my children that lying is always wrong but assume they won't hear that small fib I told over the phone to someone who was asking for some of my precious time.

When Tim blows up over some minor incident I lecture him on the uselessness of his anger, but a short time later I fly into a rage over a broken glass (conveniently forgetting that I break at least one glass a day).

While I preach daily (make that hourly) about keeping the house clutter picked up, I leave my coat, shoes, books, and writings lying all over the house.

Lord, I need to get my own act in order so I can be a good example to my children.

Many non-Christians attribute their skepticism to the behavior of hypocritical Christians. I don't believe that's a good excuse. Nevertheless, I don't want to be the reason for my children to reject You.

Change me, Lord, into Your image. Help me not just to confess and accept Your forgiveness for these sins but to work harder at changing my bad habits. Let Your Spirit remind me of the right response before I open my big mouth.

You have set the perfect example for me, Your

daughter. When I grow up, I want to be just like You.

> Let your light so shine before men that they may see your good works and give glory to your Father who is in heaven.
>
> Matthew 5:16

You hypocrite, first take the log out of your own eye, and then you will see clearly to take the speck out of your brother's eye.

Matthew 7:5

Vanity, Vanity

Father, don't You think my children are carrying this good-grooming act too far?

I knew I'd have to make sacrifices for them, but I didn't know I'd have to bathe and wash my hair in cold water and take the last place in line for the bathroom every morning. By the time I get a turn at the blow dryer it shuts off from being overheated! I'm getting a little tired of going to work with damp hair.

It seems like just yesterday that I had to bribe my boys to get them into the bathtub; now in order to get them out I have to threaten to call in the National Guard.

The bathroom countertop which I once could see is now covered with an array of face cleansers, scrubs, acne lotion, blush, eyelash curler, lip gloss, barrettes and clips, medicated soap, combs, brushes, razors, shaving lotions, three different kinds of toothpaste, toothbrushes, mouthwash, shampoo, hair conditioner, wet washrags and towels, and the blower dryer and curling iron (which is left on most of the day). Oh, yes, back there in the corner under a towel is my makeup case.

The long counter and mirror are helpful. Several people could stand in there side by side and coexist peacefully—that is, if they were not siblings.

Lord, I don't remember being as picky about my appearance as they are about theirs. I did wash my face a lot and try to steam and press out my blackheads. I also put my hair in pin curls or rollers every night.

All right, I admit it. I was as vain then as my own kids are now.

Here I was just a few years ago asking for Your help in getting them to pay some attention to their appearance. I'm never satisfied, am I?

Help my children to be as concerned about their inner cleanliness as they are about their exterior.

And give me enough patience to endure until they move out and have their very own bathrooms.

The Lord rewarded me according to my righteousness; according to the cleanness of my hands he recompensed me.

Psalm 18:20

Create in me a clean heart, O God, and put a new and right spirit within me.

Psalm 51:10

Individuals

Lord, let me treat each of my children as the unique separate persons that they are.

I have made mistakes in the past by expecting the same accomplishments from them. That's unfair of me.

They have let me know when I am guilty of this transgression.

"I'm not Gene!" Tim said when he quit band and piano lessons over my objections. I realized then that I had to let Tim be himself and follow his own interests. His hobby of collecting comic books is his own specialty, and I respect it.

Lana too insists on her own field of activities. She enjoys singing and sports.

I need to be more careful to avoid grouping my children together in one lump. Keep me from expecting identical academic interests and abilities from them.

They are at an age when they sometimes compare themselves with others and form the conclusions that their achievements are not as important as someone else's. My daughter often complains that she does not excel at any one thing. You and I know that's not so. Help her and her brothers to understand they they're unique and special, and that I love them for what and who they are rather than for what they do.

I wouldn't like it much if I thought You expected me to match the talents of each of my friends. You have distributed Your gifts among us all. Help us to recognize, accept, and develop the talents You have given us, and not waste our time trying to duplicate someone else's life.

Thank You for making us individuals and for loving us as we are.

. . . because you are precious in my eyes, and honored, and I love you.
Isaiah 43:4a

Unaccomplished Deceivers

My kids are lousy liars, Lord.

I didn't have to take a course in body language to be able to read them. They each have their own signals which flash the message "It's a lie" to me.

Gene's eyes shift up, down, and all around when he's evading the truth. As a young child he was amazed by my ability to tell when he was lying. In later years he was annoyed by my perception and became defensive whenever my assessment hit home. He informs me now that I wasn't always right, but won't issue any exact statistics on my accuracy.

Tim has great difficulty getting a lie to come out of his mouth. If he's backed into a corner he either tells the truth or states in no uncertain terms that he does not wish to talk about it.

A slight smile or indignation betrays any fibs Lana may make. I'm sure You remember that one occasion when her conscience forced her to confess to a deed that she and her brothers had conspired to cover up. While my husband and I were out one evening a large decorative ashtray that was on the coffee table was broken. When I asked what had happened the children all claimed they didn't know. Soon afterward Lana came downstairs in tears to confess she had done it. Lord, wasn't it neat that it bothered her enough to confess? I was also impressed that Gene then insisted that they were all to blame, since they were playing with her jump rope when it happened.

The ashtray was incidental; it could be replaced. Their honesty made me feel that they have absorbed some of the values I've been pushing. I'm glad they're not accomplished at telling falsehoods. It gives me assurance that their sense of right and wrong is still intact.

They are often a conscience for Willard and me. I think twice about using false excuses to get out of a meeting or social commitment. I'm intimidated by their disapproving looks when they hear me lie.

I thank You, Lord, for this indication that I'm not a complete failure in this mission to guide my children toward responsible adulthood.

Forgive my children's lies, and also my own, in the name of the One who is truth.

Set a guard over my mouth, O Lord; keep watch over the door of my lips.

Psalm 141:3

Put away from you crooked speech, and put devious talk far from you. Let your eyes look directly forward, and your gaze be straight before you.

Proverbs 4:24,25

Travel Trauma

Lord, why can't my family enjoy vacations together?

Planning regular annual trips has always been difficult because of our family business. Except for a few occasions, the best we've been able to manage is a weekend trip every once in a while. Shorter periods of car confinement do result in better dispositions.

Until our trip to San Francisco three years ago, I thought that traveling together would be easier when the children got older. I had such high expectations for that three-day vacation!

Since our family had been divided most of that summer, I decided that this trip to the Bay Area was necessary to pull us back together. What a disaster! Everyone had his own idea of an itinerary. Gene wanted to check out the music stores for different sheet music; Tim had a list of comic-book collector's stores; Lana and I were anxious to go shopping; and Willard didn't really want to be there at all (too much traffic and confusion). We tried to work it all into our schedule, but whoever was waiting for his turn was impatient. The family closeness I had anticipated was like the sour candies my kids eat.

Confinement in the car for 300 miles with four tall, long-legged people, a teenage driver who resented any comments about his driving, and two other children who couldn't look at each other without fighting was quite an experience. At one point Gene stopped the car, got out, and started walking down the freeway, and I had to go after him and talk him back into the car. We argued about every detail—when and where to eat, where to stay, etc.

Now here I am again planning a two-week vacation for this summer. Once again I have great hopes of it being a relaxing, fun time for us all. Since our oldest child will not be with us and the other two are now three years older, I am hesitantly confident that it will be a pleasant vacation.

Of course, there is a possible conflict with two young drivers; and they're already asking why we can't spend all our time in one of the big cities instead of going back to Montana to visit relatives. On second thought. . . .

Lord, my family is shrinking, and I feel like we haven't had nearly enough time to be together. I'm looking forward to a couple of weeks without work, housework, and school schedules.

Help us to get along this summer and enjoy each other's company. Assist us in planning this trip so that it doesn't become another trap of schedules. Keep us flexible in our commitments so that we can relax and have fun (no matter how much it hurts).

I expect us to have a terrific time.

There I go again.

Oh, well, life would be terribly boring without dreams.

> Commit your work to the Lord, and your plans will be established.
>
> Proverbs 16:3

> You shall go out in joy and be led forth in peace; the mountains and hills before you shall break forth into singing, and all the trees of the field shall clap their hands.
>
> Isaiah 55:12

It's Really Happening!

Can it be, Lord? Do I see signs of maturity in my oldest son's character?

Since coming home from a term away at college, he has exhibited an unusual fondness for being part of the family. For a few years there he acted like we didn't exist (except as a 24-hour favor-handout machine). He's been staying home on weekends now. Weekend nights have been tame also. When he stayed home last Saturday night I thought I was hallucinating. I even heard him turn down an invitation to go to a party.

His sudden attentiveness to his brother and sister amaze me. He has been chauffering them around with no complaints. He has been playing chess with Tim every night and even talked Tim into going golfing with him. The most pleasant surprise was what he did for Lana on her birthday. He insisted on taking her around to try on jeans and bought her a cute pink pair of overalls. In addition to this present he took her out to lunch.

Lord, if I'm dreaming, please don't wake me.

Friends had been telling me to hang on—that a change was just around the corner—but I couldn't believe them. I thought they were inventing hope to cheer me up.

I'm ashamed of my lack of faith. If I'd been trying to walk on water I'd have drowned long ago.

Forgive my lack of confidence in You, me, and Gene.

Thank You for Your faithfulness. It causes my heart to shout out with joy:

LOOK, EVERYBODY, MY SON IS GROWING UP!

I will give thanks to the Lord with my whole heart; I will tell of all thy wonderful deeds. I will be glad and exult in thee; I will sing praise to thy name, O Most High.

Psalm 9:1,2

Jesus immediately reached out his hand and caught him, saying to him, "O man of little faith, why did you doubt?"

Matthew 14:31

The Scapegoat

Father, almost everything that's wrong with the world today is blamed on TV.

Isn't that marvelous? Now that Satan has been written off as a mere symbol of the evil in the world, we can focus our blame where it belongs—on the "tube."

It's a common consensus that children today are listless, bored, and unimaginative because they watch TV. It also causes them to eat the wrong foods and to drive their parents crazy by asking for the toys they see advertised. Anyone knows that they can't learn in school because teachers are unable to compete with TV. Also, any crimes they commit are attributed to some violent program they watched. There's not enough time for me to include all the sins of that square box that sits in the living room of almost every home in the country.

If the TV generation can't read, then why is Tim's room covered with wall-to-wall, ceiling-to-floor books? If they are underachievers, then why are Tim and Lana's grades always above average? I'm not bragging; I'm just trying to prove that these accusations aren't always true.

I have not censored the programs my kids watch, with two or three exceptions. Yet I find them watching the better-quality programming. Don't You think we set a precedent by our choice of shows?

Even mediocre and controversial shows can serve a good purpose by stimulating good discussions and moral teachings. With a little assistance kids can easily distinguish between the real and the phony, and they often express their opinions of how the conflict in a story could be solved.

Lord, I marvel at the capabilities You have given us to enrich our minds. Help us all to use them to enhance and upbuild our mental state.

Help my children to absorb the good in what they see and block out anything that would hinder their development as Your children.

Guide my own program selections so that my mind is only filled with thoughts that enrich my existence.

I will not set before my eyes anything that is base.

Psalm 101:3a

Finally, brethren, whatever is true, whatever is honorable, whatever is just, whatever is pure, whatever is lovely, whatever is gracious, if there is any excellence, if there is anything worthy of praise, think about these things.

Philippians 4:8

Uncensored

Lord, save my children from this sickness called pornography that is spreading throughout the country.

I become more disgusted every day by the reports of its different forms and results.

While I wouldn't want us to return to the theory that sex is evil, I deplore how far we've come. We've reached a point where we just shrug our shoulders and concede that everyone has a right to do his own thing. We shut our eyes to the fact that we are all affected, even if we don't read or watch or participate in the distortion of physical intimacy. We are the victims of our society.

It may be normal for our children to read suggestive magazines out of curiosity, but I don't think we can leave it at that. We need to point out to them what an unreal picture they are getting. Movies and TV programs and ads that exploit our sexual feelings are using us all, and I resent it.

Many young people think that love is sex and sex is love, and they marry with this false understanding. The results, of course, are unhappy and broken marriages.

The extremes are becoming sickening, yet a misunderstanding of the word "freedom" keeps us from stopping it. Who is defending the rights of those who are being sexually used and abused?

The fear of censorship is being overplayed. Taking steps to protect our children does not have to mean a return to the puritanical age. Surely there's a way to have moral reason without fanaticism.

Whatever happened to good taste?

Show us how to accomplish this, Lord; give us the courage we need to fight the princes of darkness who are trying to entrap our children.

Keep our minds and theirs free of corruption so we may enjoy the beauty of real love.

> He has delivered us from the dominion of darkness and transferred us to the kingdom of his beloved Son.
>
> Colossians 1:13

> They promise them freedom, but they themselves are slaves of corruption, for whatever overcomes a man, to that he is enslaved.
>
> 2 Peter 2:19

> Whoever causes one of these little ones who believe in me to sink it would be better for him to have a great millstone fastened round his neck and to be drowned in the depth of the sea.
>
> Matthew 18:6

Main Course—Words

Father, forgive me for any judgments I've made of other parents.

The correct approach is always easy to see when we are observing someone else's problem. I wish I could take back all those words, "Now if that were my kid. . . ."

Did I really say my toddlers would go to bed when they were told, would eat what I put in front of them, and would never whine or throw tantrums?

When I was in the midst of preschool pandemonium I envied my friends with older children. Their warnings about impending storms on the horizons fell on unbelieving ears. I was quite sure that I knew how to handle school-age children and teenagers and would breeze through those phases. I even thought I'd enjoy it.

I made mental notes along the way of what I saw other parents doing wrong. I was sure that kids who had flaws in their characters were the result of poor parenting. All around me I saw parents who were either too strict or too permissive. I vowed to treat my teenagers with love, respect, and trust, which I knew would enable us to work out any disagreement.

Such pride and arrogance! How could You keep from shaking the earth with Your laughter, Lord?

The conflicts started out slowly, with arguments over hair length and clothing. Then suddenly the atmosphere changed. I was surrounded by hostile vibrations.

Still I persisted in my mental assessments of other families. I could see that this parent didn't set enough limits, or that parent was far too picky, or another didn't spend enough time with his or her child. I knew how to solve every problem except the ones that were going on in my own household.

I couldn't understand what was happening to my rapport with my kids. They challenged my authority, disdained my heart-to-heart advice, and ignored my feelings.

I began to empathize with the parents I had been judging. Who was I to criticize others when my own children were just like theirs—normal?

Lord, I confess these sins of a superior attitude and ask Your forgiveness.

Give me the courage to approach other troubled parents with my humble heart in hand, and to share my own experiences. Together we can cry and laugh about ourselves and our families. With fewer judgments, more humor, and Your assistance we're bound to make it.

Meanwhile, our kids and You will be able to work out their lives in spite of whatever damage we have done.

And, Lord, keep me from ever again uttering, "I know what that kid's problems is; his parents should . . ."

Judge not, that you be not judged. For with the judgment you pronounce you will be judged, and the measure you give will be the measure you get.

Matthew 7:1,2

Let us no more pass judgment on one another, but rather decide never to put a stumbling block or hindrance in the way of a brother.

Romans 14:13

Holiday Dreams

Lord, holidays just aren't what they used to be!

None of my children wants to dye Easter eggs, light fireworks, carve pumpkins, or make and decorate Christmas cookies. They sure are turning boring on me!

Where did I go wrong?

I still knock myself out cooking special holiday dinners, baking special goodies for each occasion, and decorating and buying presents, but their reactions are just not the same.

They look at their chocolate hearts and bunnies and sigh,

"Mom, what are you trying to do to me? If I eat these, I'll be covered with zits!"

They're no longer interested in searching for their baskets or eggs after church on Easter. This year Tim and Lana ambled downstairs for their stockings as they awoke late on Christmas morning. Gene came by about 2:00 P.M. to check his out before we went to dinner. When we opened gifts the night before there wasn't any wild anticipation or squeals of pleasure.

I shouldn't complain. It was certainly more pleasant than some other holidays we've spent together. Take the one year when we had a knock-down-drag-out fight with out oldest because he planned to wear his stocking hat to church. Or a Thanksgiving when an argument started and Gene stormed out just before dinner. Shortly afterward my husband left the same way, and three of us sat down to a quiet dinner which I cried through.

Do these scenes happen in other homes, Lord? How do other women handle them?

I have sometimes accepted invitations for dinner out or invited people in partly because I know we will be on our best behavior in front of others. After all, we must play the part of the happy American family!

Thank You for the more recent holidays when we have put aside our differences and enjoyed each other's company. I'll accept that even if I would prefer a little more enthusiasm.

Father, help me to adjust to my children's changing ages. I can't keep them from growing up and away from family traditions or control their actions toward one another. I can accept what we have and stop expecting holidays to be a cure-all for every little annoyance.

Help us to put aside our criticisms for those few days a year at least. The outer wrappings are not important. Being together is.

Thank You for these years when we are still all together. Help us to appreciate each other now, before we get too far away.

Whether you eat or drink or whatever you do, do all to the glory of God.

1 Corinthians 10:31

Leaving Home

Father, I'm sorry I wasn't here to help my son move out today.

My emotions were so mixed and close to the surface that I was afraid he'd think I'd finally cracked. When I talked to him later on the phone I still could not talk without tears in my voice.

My mind tells me that this step is necessary for his own growth, but my heart cries, "Come back! Don't go!"

I thought I had prepared myself for this moment. I guess I was more prepared for a joyous leave-taking. The fact that he was retreating from a battleground made his leaving harder to bear. However, he may have needed this motivation to go. Perhaps if there had been no conflict he would have stayed home indefinitely. I doubt that I could handle that.

So I'll dry my tears and try to make this transition easier for him. I'll give him extra linens and dishes and furniture and answer his questions about cooking. Then I'll stand back and give him the space he needs.

Our relationship will never be what it once was. It can't be and it shouldn't be. He's no longer my little boy; he's my grown son, my younger friend.

It is somewhat quieter in the evenings with one less person arguing over the TV program selections. That one particular corner will be free of his pop cans, mail, glasses,etc. However, I miss our late-night conversations that covered every subject conceivable. As I listened to his hopes and fears about the future and some of the feelings he has just begun to share, I found myself liking him again. (You know, for a while there I loved him, but didn't always like him.)

Now perhaps our relationship will not be hampered by nit-picky, day-today irritations.

Help me, Lord, to accept this new era in my life. I think in many ways I will enjoy my son more now that we can be together by choice. Lord, thank You for being the kind of parent who gives the love that frees us to grow. Help me to do the same.

All your sons shall be taught by the Lord, and great shall be the prosperity of your sons.

Isaiah 54:13

Worry, Worry!

Father, I can't stop worrying about these kids of mine!

You know I had never been a worrier until the children hit their teens. Now I can't seem to stop.

I kneel here before You every day and share my fears; but I take them back when my prayer is ended.

I advise them to loosen up and stop fretting. Then I stay awake stewing over their safety, their emotional well-being, their physical comforts, etc., etc.

I really do trust You to love my children and watch over them. However, I know that You have given them the freedom of making their own choices, and I am afraid they may make some mistakes that will cause them to suffer.

Do I care too much? I used to think it was never possible to overdo love. Now I wonder if I'm stifling them with love and hindering their normal development. I don't want to be a mother who smothers her children.

"Mother, don't worry," they tell me.

"Mom, maybe you shouldn't care so much."

Perhaps I do need to move back a little. By standing too close I experience every hurt they do. I could go crazy if I keep this up.

I knew I'd gone too far last week when I called my son on the phone to tell him there was black ice on the road. He just sighed and said, "Mom!" That said it all.

I'm not ecstatic about this rumor I've heard that a mother can never quit worrying about her children.

When I'm 83 will I call up my children and tell them to dress warmly? I hope not!

One woman told me that it just gets worse, since you acquire more people to worry about when your family expands to include sons-in-law and daughters-in-law and grandchildren.

Obviously some concern is necessary, but I'm getting too extreme.

Forgive me for this seeming lack of faith, and help me to trade this heavy burden of anxiety for the lighter one that You offer. My anxious thoughts produce nothing except harmful physical effects.

I bring my children to You in prayer right now and will leave them in Your able hands.

> God is our refuge and strength, a very present help in trouble. Therefore we will not fear though the earth should change, though the mountains shake in the heart of the sea; though its waters roar and foam, though the mountains tremble with its tumult.
>
> Psalm 46:1-3

> Come to me, all who labor and are heavy-laden, and I will give you rest. Take my yoke upon you, and learn from me; for I am gentle and lowly in heart, and you will find rest for your souls. For my yoke is easy, and my burden is light.
>
> Matthew 11:28-30

Which Is It?

Lord, where is the fine line between loving our children and spoiling them?

I think I crossed it long ago, and I need to find my way back. It's important for my children's sake as well as mine.

I accepted the role of permanent, year-round Santa Claus and have struggled to buy my children most of their wishes. When they were younger they received the most-popular toys. Later it was brand-name jeans and tennis shoes. While I am objecting to being used I continue to hand out car keys, the gas card, and that elusive green and white paper.

Why do I do it? I guess it's partly because I want them to love me. I've never admitted that before. I thought I did these things because I love them.

Lately I find that I'm not receiving anything in return for my gifts. Rather than loving me for my generosity, my children complain about my inability to give them more. The guilt they evoke in me causes me to sacrifice my wants for theirs. I'm beginning to feel resentful about spending most of my money on my kids. It seems like the only time they care about Mom and Dad is when they want something from us.

Money and possessions are not the only ways in which we spoil our children. We also do too many things for them that they could do themselves. I've been making gradual progress in this area. My kids prepare their own food if they're not around for mealtime or don't approve of my bill of fare. Today I even refused to iron a blouse for Lana and advised her to do it herself. For a former aspiring super-mom that took courage! Although I am sometimes forced to say no to my children because of the nature of my job, they don't appear to be suffering from any deep emotional maladies. They have even shown some resourcefulness in finding their own rides after school when they are unable to catch the bus.

Lord, this is a difficult task for me. After years of letting my children sleepwalk through life, I need to wake them up and introduce them to the real world. How do I do this without hurting them? Being a parent is a puzzling occupation. Whenever we think we know the ground rules, our kids change them.

Balance my love with common sense. But, Lord, I'd rather err on the side of love than deprive my children of the feeling of being cared about.

You didn't let us flounder through life. You stretched out Your hand and offered salvation. Thank You for spoiling us with this unfathomable love.

While we were still weak, at the right time Christ died for the ungodly.

Romans 5:6

I will not leave you desolate; I will come to you.

John 14:18

The Lord upholds all who are falling, and raises up all who are bowed down. The eyes of all look to thee, and thou givest them their food in due season. Thou openest thy hand, thou satisfiest the desire of every living thing.

Psalm 145:14-16

Welcome to the Zoo

Lord, You don't have to be crazy to live here, but it helps.

If I were in control of my faculties I certainly would not have been here in this living room tonight sitting on my daughter's feet while she did her nightly sit-ups, and listening and interpreting Macbeth for my son.

I was hoping for some quiet time this weekend, when everyone would leave and I· could get the house in some semblance of order and plow through the pile of bills, mail, and tax forms on my desk. However, my husband and sons could't get together on when to go to work at the shop, so they were underfoot most of the time.

My husband decided to make a big pot of soup and left the kitchen looking like it had been vandalized. Gene spent an hour taking inventory of our freezer and asking for various items to take back to his apartment. Tim had the small figurines he was painting spread out all over the table. Lana and her friends ran in and out asking for the car every half-hour—to go to the store for toothpaste, to drive to the tennis courts (three blocks away), to go after a soft pretzel, to get a magazine.

This is a typical Sunday afternoon at our home. The only peace I enjoy is the hour I spend with you in church, and late at night, when the mob has settled down.

Both my boys have recently studied family living in school and haven't been able to figure out what category to put our family in.

"This family is weird," they both concluded.

"The word is *unique*," I insisted.

Father, it's easy to thank You for this family when everything is running smoothly. I thank You also for these zany, wonderful, dumb moments that hopefully can never be relived. Keep these moments in my memory as a shield for the spears that often attack my heart.

Help us to smile more. After all, if You didn't want us to laugh You wouldn't have put us all together in our family.

> The Lord is good to all, and his compassion is over all that he has made.

> Psalm 145:9

> Pray for the peace of Jerusalem! May they prosper who love you! Peace be within your walls, and security within your towers!

> Psalm 122:6,7

The Overcomers

Father, how can I bolster up my children's self-images?

When they were younger a few words of praise and a hug gave them assurance that they were important. The task is much harder today.

They are dissatisfied with their appearances and refuse to believe that they are or ever will be attractive. They set high goals for their school grades and berate themselves for receiving anything less than an A.

They sigh in disbelief when I praise their performance in concerts or programs. I can hear them thinking, What does she know? She's just my mother.

I never claimed to be an unbiased critic. After all, they're my kids. They're the best!

Although they do not seem to accept my approval as conclusive, they continue to ask for it.

"How did you like that number, Mom?"

"Does this dress look all right?"

"Mom, I got an A in my final."

I need to be careful in my choice of words even when we're kidding around. Their feelings are tender despite their indifferent act.

It's taken me years to accept myself, and I'm sure it will be a while before my children are confident of themselves.

Lord, let me do whatever I can to help them to that end. Then take over and guide them to love themselves and You.

Thank You for loving us even when we don't love ourselves.

He drew me up from the desolate pit, out of the miry bog, and set my feet upon a rock, making my steps secure.

Psalm 40:2

Whatever is born of God overcomes the world; and this is the victory that overcomes the world, our faith. Who is it that overcomes the world but he who believes that Jesus is the Son of God?

1 John 5:4,5

Enigma

Lord, being a parent is so confusing!

If we pay close attention to our children and are concerned about every aspect of their lives, we are labeled as overprotective.

However, if we back off and let them grow up naturally, we are accused of being neglectful.

I've been trying to maintain a middle position, but I'm being pulled back and forth like a tug-of-war rope.

Long ago I decided that I did not want mealtime to be a battle of wills. Therefore I provided good food and let the children choose. I had read somewhere that even if they lived on peanut-butter sandwiches they would not die of malnutrition. This attitude has been fairly successful. The children have added many foods to their diet and now even eat some vegetables. But there's a critic lurking in the deep recesses of my mind that keeps whispering that I'm not a very good mother because I don't force my children to always eat well-balanced meals.

I found myself in the same dilemma over music lessons. I wanted them to learn to play because they wanted to, not because I forced them. However, I have been told by other parents that their children excelled in music because the parents made sure they practiced every day without fail.

Child-care and psychological books present both views. Which expert is the expert, Lord?

I have come to the conclusion that there are no

absolutes when it comes to children. I know I should have understood that way back when I was going through the bottle-to-cup weaning and potty-training stages. Have patience with me, Lord. I'm a slow learner.

All these conflicting views that are floating around cause me to seriously doubt my success as a parent. Have I been too strict in some areas and too permissive in others? What could I have done differently?

I don't know what I can do except to be myself and trust my feelings. If I tried to play it tough, my kids would probably laugh themselves sick. I would also get a strange reaction if I suddenly dropped the few rules I insist upon.

Recently my daughter made my heart soar when she remarked that I was a good "in-between mother" because I let them go where they want to most of the time but care enough to make them tell me where they're going and what they're doing.

Not too long ago, when I threatened to "go mod," my son said, "You're all right the way you are." I almost fell out of my chair.

What do you think, Lord? How am I doing?

I know I've made mistakes. I hope they have not permanently damaged the mental health of my children.

Guide me along the fence of reason, Lord, and control my reactions to my children's behavior. Help me to neither overreact nor underreact.

Only with Your help can I trust my own mind. Fill me with wisdom and logic, and temper me with love. Then I will put the rest in Your capable hands.

After all, they are Your children too.

Why do I keep forgetting that?

> I will instruct you and teach you the way you should go.
>
> Psalm 32:8

Don't Eat What I Eat

Father, if I've told these kids once I've told them a thousand times that they need to eat a more balanced diet.

Their eating habits are atrocious. They skip breakfast and/or lunch and eat everything in sight when they get home from school. Then they're already full and won't eat supper. If they have money in their pockets and don't like what I'm fixing, they head for the nearest fast-food place.

They refuse to believe me when I tell them that not eating properly or consuming sugar and cola drinks is making them tired. As usual, they think Mom doesn't know what she's talking about.

Recently my oldest son went to the doctor about stomachaches and was told what he should not be eating and drinking. He has avoided those foods faithfully. But he could have paid me for the same advice! Now that he has been a less-frequent visitor at the hamburger joints and has watched what he eats, his skin is beginning to clear up at last. (And he told me for years that his diet had no effect on his acne!)

Lord, I often despair of telling these kids anything, since they act like I'm just a babbling, brainless old lady. I guess they'll find out someday that I'm usually right.

I haven't been a very good example when it comes to nutrition, since I don't practice it very well myself. I always have good intentions of maintaining a well-balanced diet so I can lose this excess weight and feel better. But You know how it is. I don't have time in the morning to do more than swing by the store and get a donut to gulp down. At lunch I do better, but by afternoon break I have a candy bar, cookies, or cola. Then I'm often tired when I get home, and I cook a lopsided meal and eat too much. I guess it isn't hard to see where my kids picked up their lousy eating habits. Kids always seem to hear what we do rather than what we say!

Help me, Lord, to give up these foods that are harming my body and to control my emotional impulses toward sweets as a security blanket. There are times when my craving for sugar equals the uncontrollable thirst of an alcoholic. I need Your strength to break this addictive pattern of eating. Perhaps if I can get my own body in shape I'll have a right to lecture my kids.

Feed me and my children with Your spiritual food—that fills us up, not out.

> Jesus said to them, "My food is to do the will of him who sent me, and to accomplish his work."
>
> John 4:34

> Jesus said to them, "I am the bread of life; he who comes to me shall not hunger, and he who believes in me shall never thirst."
>
> John 6:35

Bedside Manners

Father, I'm not a very good nurse.

I've never been a hovering, chicken-soup-type mother. I guess I've been afraid that if I doted too much my kids would get the impression that being sick was more fun than school!

We've suffered extended bouts of the flu some winters, but spring always eradicates the germs of sickness, along with the gloom. I haven't had to deal with any serious illnesses so my worries seem inconsequential. Still, even these minor ailments are distressing.

When our children were babies we felt helpless because they were unable to tell us what hurt. Now that they can express themselves it's not much better. I felt utterly helpless that winter when Tim had strep throat four times and burning stomach pains from worrying about the time he missed from school. It was the same when Lana had one cold after another last winter.

The kids have no more patience with sickness than I do. They are unwilling to miss school and make up work. Therefore they go to school even if they are slightly ill.

Lord, I need to outwardly show my children that I am concerned when they are sick. All too often I nag them about their treatment instead of expressing my inner feelings. They get the impression I don't care.

"If you'd wear a coat this wouldn't have happened," I say. "Just rest and take your pills if you want to get well. No, you're not dying!"

I sound like I'm just annoyed because I have to take care of them.

We all have a need to know that someone cares about our health. It's as necessary to our recovery as modern medicine.

My older son calls me to tell me when he's feeling sick. He seems to be asking me to worry about him.

Lord, help me to be a better nurse to my family when they are ill. Give me the patience I need to attend to their needs with tender, loving care.

Thank You for caring and extending Your healing hand to each of us. Hasten the coming of spring!

The prayer of faith will save the sick man.

James 5:15a

Pray for one another, that you may be healed.

James 5:16b

Say What?

Lord, I often get the feeling that we have five transmitters in this family but no receivers.

Doesn't this violate a fundamental law of communication?

When I'm giving a recount of the highlights of my day at work, Lana looks around the room and hums while Willard picks up the paper or silently moves his lips as he works out a math problem in his head. I feel like our TV set often runs just to provide background noise. If I trick them by adding a question to the end of my narration, I get blank stares. I know they're wondering if they should take a chance and say yes, or else admit they haven't heard a word I've said.

Without a receiver it's impossible to tell when someone else is broadcasting. Therefore transmission signals are often garbled from interference. The other day I adjusted my fine tuner and tried to interpret what was being said. This is what I heard:

"Mom, I have to . . ."

"I got an A on my . . ."

"be at school . . ."

"Dad, what day . . ."

". . . math final."

". . . early tomorrow."

"Where . . ."

"are we going to . . ."

"is the TV schedule?"

The communication lines in this household are so crammed with inconsequential chitchat that our feelings never get through. It's frustrating when our kids clam up. It sometimes causes us to claim the power to interpret their thoughts.

I want better communication in our family, not so that I can make my children concur with my opinions (although that would be nice), but because I really want to know what they're feeling.

Help us, Lord, to listen when our children open up, and to respond with love and understanding. Perhaps they would express their feelings more often if they were not afraid of our responses. Open the ears to their hearts, and also help them to listen to our feelings.

Help us not to try to control our children under the guise of communication.

Thank You, Lord, for listening to my transmissions. Keep my antennae ready to receive Your answers.

Give heed to my reproof; behold, I will . . . make my words known to you.

Proverbs 1:23

A fool takes no pleasure in understanding, but only in expressing his opinion.

Proverbs 18:2

Take Not My Sons!

Father, I don't want my sons to go to war.

You probably hear this same prayer from every mother in the world.

It isn't fair to be asked to send our young men (or women) to kill or be killed after we've spent 18 years nurturing them.

I love my country in spite of all its faults, and I truly believe we have to protect it and try to spread our ideals to other countries. But I'm not willing to sacrifice my children!

I've taught them to be tolerant of people of all colors, religions, and nationalities. How can I expect them to fight other people to prove that our way is right?

Is it any wonder that our young people see hypocrisy in our religion? It's hard to explain why DO NOT KILL does not apply to a person whom our government decides is our enemy. That person is a living child of Yours, with the same hopes and dreams as my children.

You know how diligently I have tried to teach my children nonviolence. I have lectured them extensively on the futility of physical force.

"Fighting never solves anything," I've told them again and again as I pulled them apart. "The real man is the one who refuses to fight, but solves the problem with brainpower. In the long run he's the brave one. It takes more courage to abstain."

Then came the test of my teaching. I hated the fistfights and rock-browing battles my sons engaged in. They each reacted in their own way. Gene tried to avoid fights and even took beatings without trying to defend himself. This made him a target for boys who were caught up in the trap of proving how tough they were. Remember how I cried for his vindication? I wanted to take the principles back and tell him to get out there and beat those brats up.

Tim didn't seem to suffer so much. Although he didn't start fights, he made it clear that he would defend himself well if he had to.

Their attitudes have carried through to the present. Gene feels strongly that war is senseless and is not the answer to the differences between countries. Tim feels that war may sometimes be necessary, and that a person should fight if it is.

I recall a history teacher of mine saying that instead of spending money for weapons we should be sending our young people to visit young people in other countries so they would not want to shoot at one another. I thoroughly agree, but unfortunately the old men still pull the strings, and they are still caught up in the quest to prove honor and valor by these inane tests of strength called war.

Lord, I reject the notion that You approve of war. Do not boys on every side of these conflicts ask for Your blessing and protection?

Help us to find other means to reach agreements. Show us how to defend human rights without refusing them to someone else.

Give my sons and daughter the wisdom they need to make a decision they can live with and courage to stand by whatever choice they make about the armed services. There have been times when I have encouraged joining in order to obtain an ordered disciplined way of life. However, when I remember what it trains them for, I shudder.

Lord, guide us as a nation toward a climate of peace and understanding toward other countries.

Help us to remember that, although we may despise oppressive forms of government, we cannot help by killing the people. I know we must defend ourselves, but I pray that we will do so only when there is no alternative. Shower us with alternatives, Lord, that our sons and daughters may be free from the threat of war, yet live under a system of government that respects each individual's liberty.

Our nation is far from being perfect, but please don't give up on us yet. We're trying.

Peace is just beyond the next hill, or the next one, or the next one.

> He shall judge between the nations, and shall decide for many people; and they shall beat their swords into plowshares, and their spears into pruning hooks; nation shall not lift up sword against nation, neither shall they learn war any more.
>
> Isaiah 2:4

> Jesus said to him, "Put your sword back into its place; for all who take the sword will perish by the sword."
>
> Matthew 26:52

Whose Grade Is It?

Father, who is responsible for my children's grades?

This theory may be radical and startling. I believe that my children are responsible for their own grades.

They know I'm always available to help them when I can. However, I will not be forced into the role of slave driver. If they don't do their homework, *they* will receive the F, not I.

I may have the power to make them stay home, turn off the TV, and sit down in front of their books, but I can't force them to learn anything. Even if I checked their homework and had them correct it and made sure they took it to school, I couldn't compel them to hand it in or pass their tests.

Father, I feel sorry for parents who are wearing themselves out prodding and pushing their kids through school. Would the world end if their kids had to go to school another year or two? Or do the parents fear a loss of face among their friends?

I admit that when our oldest came close to not graduating I tried to pass that last course for him by berating him daily about his lack of discipline. You and I both know that it wasn't my nagging that made him pass. He suddenly decided that it would be embarassing for him not to graduate with his friends, so he applied his brain and accomplished his goal.

I felt it was important to make my children feel they had to stand on their own at an early age. That's why I haven't charged at the teachers who have given them lower marks than they deserved.

"Talk to your teacher about it." I said. "It's between you and her."

There have been times I have wanted to change this stand, but I'm glad now that I've remained firm.

My children have developed an ability to stand up for their rights when they think they've been wronged. They have discovered that teachers sometimes make mistakes and are willing to admit this and change a grade.

By not accepting responsibility for my children's grades, I give them the right to be proud of themselves when they do well. They deserve the good marks they get because they work hard to get them.

Stop me if I open my mouth to lecture my children about their grades. Remind me that I'm overstepping my authority. Assist them in their quest for learning. Let the knowledge be as important to them as the grades. The two are not necessarily synonymous.

If You gave out marks for my progress through life so far, I'm afraid I'd be on permanent academic probation.

Teach me again, Lord!

Wisdom will come into your heart, and knowledge will be pleasant to your soul.

Proverbs 2:10

Fear not the reproach of men, and be not dismayed at their revilings.

Isaiah 51:7b

Lift Me Back Up

Father, am I a bad specimen of Your creation?

After listening to my children's criticisms of me, I could easily conclude that nothing about me is acceptable.

My daughter reviews my singing voice in church and makes me feel like a honking goose in an angel choir.

She also scrutinizes my hair and clothing and is giving me a complex about my appearance. She gives me disparaging glances when I eat high-calorie snacks. I hesitate to buy new clothes without her approval. (Subsequently I find my new sweaters or blouses in her closet!)

As I have grown older I have become less inhibited about striking up conversations with strangers or acting silly. Tim is often embarassed by my behavior now. We seem to be switching roles.

You know what a struggle it has been to reach this point where I like myself and have confidence in the talents that You've given me. I really don't need my family to knock chips off my ego.

Perhaps their purpose is to keep me humble. Their "so what?" attitude about my writing gives me an incentive to work harder at it.

About the time I think I'm doing pretty well at being a mother, they bring me down to earth by comparing me to "someone else's mom" who spends more money than I do for her children's clothes and recreation and gives her kids more freedom.

When I begin to feel smug about my Christian

character they point out my flaws, and I come back to You to be refilled.

Are You trying to show me what I do to them when I criticize them?

Okay, Lord, I get the message. Enough!

Make me a container for Your love; pour out approval, understanding, and forbearance through me. And, Lord, could You arrange it so they give me some in return?

If it's not possible, that's all right. Your love is sufficient! It's all I need for my self-esteem.

> Do thou, O Lord, protect us; guard us ever from this generation.
> Psalm 12:7

> In return for my love they accuse me, even as I make prayer for them.
> Psalm 109:4

> He who is in you is greater than he who is in the world.
> 1 John 4:4b

Deflationomics

When, O Lord, will my children learn how to handle money?

My husband and I have been serving as a non-profit lending institution for quite some time.

When my son calls me at work during the week before payday I know instinctively what he wants.

"I need 20 dollars to get through the weekend," he explains.

"Why don't you stay home until you get the money on Monday?" I ask, knowing that it's a futile question.

"Mom! It's a weekend!"

We advise him to save some of his money when he does get paid.

"But I have to have this new album and I have bills to pay. I'll save some next time," he replies.

He and I recently discussed his inability to save and concluded that the only method that will work is if he gives it to me and I put it in an account that he can't get to. Then I will refuse to give it to him in spite of any hard-luck story he may give me.

My daughter's lack of money is often our fault. We have a running I.O.U. with her for allowances, report cards, etc., which she draws on. These draws immediately disappear for clothing, magazines, cosmetics, and other female teenage necessities!

Tim is the investor of the family. He puts his whole check into savings and then bums the money from you-know-who for his weekly minor expenses.

Lord, It's hard to let go of children with bad spending habits. Although we know we should refuse to give them extra money when they don't live within their means, we are unable to stick to our resolutions.

Perhaps this reluctance to enforce our monetary theories comes from our own inability to stick to them.

Help us all to work out of this present economic confusion. These hard times are teaching us all not to put our faith in this fleeting green-and-white mirage that we call money.

I thank You now for the help I know You will give people all across our country who are willing to work hard, change their excessive desires, and use their brains and Your power.

Money may be temporary, but Your love and the ingenuity You have given us are not. They may be temporarily hidden, but they will rise again as surely as a cork in water, and they will bob over the tops of the waves. When the sea is once more calm, we corks will still be afloat!

Thank You for caring about our material needs. Help us always to share with other people. No matter how bad our own circumstances are, there's always someone worse off whom we can help.

If I can pass these truths on to my children I won't fear their financial survival.

You are the grand prize in the sweepstakes of our lives.

He who trusts in his riches will wither, but the righteous will flourish like a green leaf.

Proverbs 11:28

He will be the stability of your times.

Isaiah 33:6

My God will supply every need of your according to his riches in glory in Christ Jesus.

Philippians 4:19

Their Earthly Father

Lord, send showers of blessing upon the father of my children. He deserves them.

In my zeal to be the perfect mother I sometimes neglect him. We differ in opinion on almost every subject except politics. However, we are committed to this marriage and our children. I can't explain why. There are times when we both doubt our capacity to endure our family, and we are thankful for the stamina You have given us. It has helped cement our love and change it from a fickle, romantic dream into a mature, enduring reality.

We each have separate dreams for our children and different ways of showing them our love. Quite often we disagree on how to handle the children. Our dissimilar attitudes are not surprising, since we are almost a generation apart in age. Also, his background as a farm boy and mine as a city girl are reflected in the expectations we have for our kids.

Our kids in their struggle to find themselves usually reject us both.

Because he reacts to most situations first with his head, the kids and I do not always recognize his hidden love. He may not show his feelings as we would like, but we know he cares.

Show us how to convey our love to him. He's a lot more than a checkbook to us. Where would we be without his practical expertise, mechanical abilities, and strange sense of humor? Our children may get angry about his lectures and conservative opinions, but they know that when they really need him he'll always come through for them.

Help us to understand, forgive, and love this man as You do. We thank You that he continues to love and forgive us.

You have blessed our family these past 22 years as we have experienced joy, sorrow, pain, pleasure, and worry.

Thank You for being our Father and continuing to put up with our childish ways.

> If I speak in the tongues of men and of angels, but have not love, I am a noisy gong or clanging cymbal.
>
> 1 Corinthians 13:1

> Love is patient and kind; love is not jealous or boastful; it is not arrogant or rude.
>
> 1 Corinthians 13:4,5a

> Every good endowment and every perfect gift is from above, coming down from the Father of lights, with whom there is not variation or shadow due to change.
>
> James 1:17